Investigation, Analysis, and Testing of Self-Contained Oxygen Generators

NASA Technical Reports Server
(NTRS), et al., Christopher P. Keddy

The BiblioGov Project is an effort to expand awareness of the public documents and records of the U.S. Government via print publications. In broadening the public understanding of government and its work, an enlightened democracy can grow and prosper. Ranging from historic Congressional Bills to the most recent Budget of the United States Government, the BiblioGov Project spans a wealth of government information. These works are now made available through an environmentally friendly, print-on-demand basis, using only what is necessary to meet the required demands of an interested public. We invite you to learn of the records of the U.S. Government, heightening the knowledge and debate that can lead from such publications.

Included are the following Collections:

Budget of The United States Government	Code of Federal Regulations
Presidential Documents	Congressional Documents
United States Code	Economic Indicators
Education Reports from ERIC	Federal Register
GAO Reports	Government Manuals
History of Bills	House Journal
House Rules and Manual	Privacy act Issuances
Public and Private Laws	Statutes at Large

National Aeronautics and
Space Administration

Document No.   WSTF-IR-1129-001-08
Date   December 10, 2008

Investigation, Analysis, and Testing of Self-contained Oxygen Generators

Lyndon B. Johnson Space Center
White Sands Test Facility
PO Box 20
Las Cruces, NM 88004
(575) 524-5011

Preface

Self Contained Oxygen Generators (SCOGs) have widespread use in providing emergency breathing oxygen in a variety of environments including mines, submarines, spacecraft, and aircraft. These devices have definite advantages over storing of gaseous or liquid oxygen. The oxygen is not generated until a chemical briquette containing a chlorate or perchlorate oxidizer and a solid metallic fuel such as iron is ignited starting a thermal decomposition process allowing gaseous oxygen to be produced. These devices are typically very safe to store, easy to operate, and have primarily only a thermal hazard to the operator that can be controlled by barriers or furnaces. Tens of thousands of these devices are operated worldwide every year without major incident. This report examines the rare case of a SCOG whose behavior was both abnormal and lethal.

This particular type of SCOG reviewed is nearly identical to a flight qualified version of SCOG slated for use on manned space vehicles. This Investigative Report is a compilation of a National Aeronautics and Space Administration effort in conjunction with other interested parties including military and aerospace to understand the causes of the particular SCOG accident and what preventative measures can taken to ensure this incident is not repeated.

This report details the incident and examines the root causes of the observed SCOG behavior from forensic evidence. A summary of chemical and numerical analysis is provided as a background to physical testing of identical SCOG devices. The results and findings of both small scale and full scale testing are documented on a test-by-test basis along with observations and summaries. Finally, conclusions are presented on the findings of this investigation, analysis, and testing along with suggestions on preventative measures for any entity interested in the safe use of these devices.

The following authors and contributors to this investigative report are acknowledged: Christopher P. Keddy, NASA Test and Evaluation Contract (NTEC), White Sands Test Facility (WSTF); Jon P. Haas, NASA WSTF Laboratories Office; and Larry Starritt, NTEC, WSTF.

Approved by: _____
Jon P. Haas
NASA WSTF Laboratories Office

Contents

Figures

Figures (continued)

Figures (continued)

Abbreviations

ANFO	Ammonium Nitrate and Fuel Oil
BLEVE	Boiling Liquid Expanding Vapor Explosion
$C_{14}H_{30}$	Tetradecane
CEA	Chemical Equilibrium with Applications
DDT	Deflagration to Detonation Transition
EDS	Energy Dispersive X-ray Spectroscopy
FMEA	Failure Modes and Effects Analysis
FT-IR	Fourier Transform Infrared
ISS	International Space Station
$KCLO_4$	Potassium Perchlorate
KNO_3	Potassium Nitrate
L	Liter
NaCl	Sodium Chloride
$NaClO_3$	Sodium Chlorate
NOx	Mixed Oxides of Nitrogen
NTEC	NASA Test and Evaluation Contract
PSI	Pounds per Square Inch
SN	Serial Number
SCF	Standard Cubic Feet
SCOG	Self-contained Oxygen Generator
SEM	Scanning Electron Microscopy
SFOG	Solid Fuel Oxygen Generator
STP	Standard Temperature and Pressure
TC	Test Conductor
TNT	Trinitrotoluene
VCE	Vapor Cloud Explosion
WSTF	White Sands Test Facility

1.0   Introduction

This report summarizes the major findings of an investigation into the anomalous behavior of a self-contained oxygen generator (SCOG), generically referred to as an "oxygen candle" or solid fuel oxygen generator (SFOG). The particular behavior under examination was an event involving a commercially available SCOG during first use, resulting in an unexpected hazardous energetic event. When this particular SCOG was activated, a runaway reaction occurred. The result was an explosion resulting in destructive overpressure, fragmentation, thermal damage, and loss of life. The details of this event can be found in the official Board of Inquiry report (BOI 2008) regarding the SCOG accident on board the Royal Navy submarine HMS Tireless in March 2007.

The historical use of a SCOG has shown these devices are typically very safe methods of producing breathable oxygen under a wide variety of operating environments including mines, submarines, and spacecraft. The base principle of operation is that an alkali metal chlorate or perchlorate (typically sodium, lithium, or potassium) undergoes an exothermic reaction that decomposes the chlorate liberating oxygen gas in a controlled and predictable manner. The majority of SCOGs used in naval service use sodium chlorate with additional iron powder as fuel to sustain the exothermic reaction. The resulting combustion and decomposition forms three principle products: a salt, a metal oxide, and oxygen gas. The combustion rate is relatively slow, resembling the combustion process in ordinary candles. The decomposition of the chlorate yields gaseous oxygen suitable for breathing when passed through a filtration medium to remove trace undesirable products (e.g., chlorine). The candle is typically burned in a closed furnace or self-contained canister. The furnaces and canisters are insulated and isolated to maintain heat sufficient to keep the reaction proceeding while protecting the user from the heat generated.

The SCOG under investigation here is of the self-contained type that includes a sodium chlorate and iron powder mixture in brick form, used to provide ~ 2600 L (92 standard cubic feet (scf))[1] of breathable oxygen with a burn time of ~60 min. The combustion occurs in a stainless steel canister, and this canister is secured into a rack or holder to ensure the candle remains in place during operation and protects personnel from heat.

NASA is particularly interested in this specific type of SCOG since the design is nearly identical to one proposed for use in a backup oxygen generator system for manned space flight and is manufactured by the same company.

The testing and analysis presented in this report was conducted at NASA Johnson Space Center White Sands Test Facility (WSTF), Las Cruces, New Mexico, USA.

2.0   Objectives

The objectives of this investigation are outlined as follows:

1. Determine the most likely cause or causes of the anomalous behavior leading to the accident.
2. Examine available evidence for clues into the exact nature of the cause and failure mode of the SCOG.
3. Analyze the system via numerical, analytical, and empirical methods to describe the reaction based on assumptions derived from evidence and reports.
4. Attempt to recreate the event as closely as possible under controlled conditions.
5. Report findings and draw conclusions on available evidence.

---

[1] Volume is based on Standard Temperature and Pressure (STP) conditions (air at 60 °F (520 °R) and 14.696 psia (15.6°C, 1 atm).

3.0   Background

The specific details of the SCOG and the event under investigation are presented here. The SCOG device is described along with normal operation for this specific device. A brief summary of the accident is also provided.

A SCOG is sometimes referred to as an oxygen candle whose purpose is to provide an emergency supply of breathable oxygen from the combustion of a chlorate oxidizer and suitable fuel. The particular SCOG of this investigation is a SCOG26, developed and marketed by Molecular Products, Ltd., Thaxted, Essex, England. The SCOG26 oxygen candle is shown in Figure 1.

Figure 1
SCOG26 (Photo Copyright Molecular Products, Ltd., U.K.)

The SCOG26 name is partially derived from the oxygen generation capability of the candle. The "26" refers to the 2600 L of oxygen gas at standard temperature and pressure (STP) that the candle will normally produce over the course of operation. The standard burn time for this type of device can vary depending on environmental conditions, but is typically on the order of 45 to 60 min. This reaction rate produces a maximum gas generation rate of roughly 1 L/s (0.0353 scf/s) under normal operating conditions.

A generic cross-section view of the SCOG26 is shown in Figure 2. The bulk of the system is comprised of candle brick material. The brick material is ignited via an igniter cartridge (typically a .410 caliber cartridge containing black powder) inserted into the top of the SCOG26 and secured in place by a screw-on striker pin assembly. The striker is operated manually and struck using the palm of the hand to drive a pin into the igniter primer. The igniter cartridge fires hot gases down a tube that has direct access to the top of the oxygen candle. The top region contains a greater percentage of iron than the bulk candle and generates more heat to ignite the next section. This ignites an iron enriched "dome" region containing ~ 30 percent iron and 70 percent chlorate. A thin layer of ~ 15 percent iron-enriched material then burns across the top of the main brick material to promote uniform combustion along the top surface area of the candle. This ignition train provides the initial thermal input, allowing the reaction to proceed into the lower iron content region (less than 8 percent) for the remainder of combustion and maintain the required temperature in excess of the decomposition temperature of the sodium chlorate (300 °C, 572 °F).

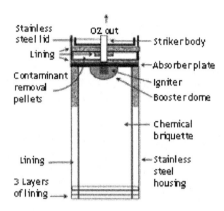

Figure 2
SCOG Cross-section Schematic (Molecular Products, Ltd.)

The SCOG26 brick material is made up of the following components per available material safety data sheets: sodium chlorate ($NaClO_3$, > 85 percent), barium peroxide (< 4 percent), and iron powder (< 8 percent). The barium peroxide is used as a chlorine scrubber.

The operation of the SCOG26 forces oxygen gas through a filter assembly located at the top of the SCOG26. The filtered oxygen then exits the SCOG26 through eight ports in the top of the canister. The filter is a mixture of manganese dioxide and copper oxide known as Hopcalite[1] (a catalyst for converting CO to CO_2, typically used in cartridge-type gas mask CO filters). The brick is insulated within the container with Kaowool[2] a high temperature aluminosilicate insulating liner material.

The primary safety feature of this SCOG26 design are two pressure relief devices located at the top of the container that help vent excess gas should the internal pressure increase beyond the normal operating pressure. The pressure rating of the pressure relief devices is not known.

4.0   Approach

The approach used in this investigation is subdivided into several categories as follows:

1. Description of Event under Investigation
2. Examination of Evidence
3. Fault Tree, Root Cause, and Failure Modes and Effects Analysis
4. Numerical Simulation and Energy Estimations
5. Small Scale Sample Testing
6. Large Scale Testing

4.1   Description of Event under Investigation

The discussion presented here is generic in nature. The information is provided to describe the event in a manner with respect to effects or observations specific to the failure and location that are deemed public knowledge for this type of event (BOI, 2008).

---

[1] Hopcalite® is a registered trademark of Mine Safety Appliances Company, Pittsburgh, Pennsylvania.
[2] Kaowool® is a registered trademark of Thermal Ceramics, Inc., Augusta, Georgia.

The event occurred within the confines of a small equipment type room containing enough space for personnel to maneuver and store materials including oxygen candles. The room itself was of metal construction for the exterior walls, while numerous partition walls of relative low strength compared to the all-metal walls were used for separation of areas. The rough dimensions of concern were ~ 8 ft (~ 2.5 m) ceiling height, and up to ~ 10 ft (~ 3 m) across and ~ 20 ft (~ 6 m) long. The volume itself was occupied by various storage cabinets, metal lockers, bulkhead-type access doors, piping systems, glass-faced pressure gauges, and work areas typical of cramped spacecraft or seagoing vessels.

The event occurred within seconds of the primary ignition of a single SCOG26. The SCOG26 in question was ignited in the same manner as previous candles had been ignited, using a manufacturer-supplied igniter cartridge and hand-operated striker assembly.

The normal operation of the SCOG26 is to ignite the brick material, and the subsequent burn produces an oxygen flow under low pressure, estimated at 10 psi (69 kPa) or less, being forced through the filter to eight exhaust ports. The typical flow rate is sufficiently low as to be nearly undetectable by human hearing, and the exiting gases are colorless. The normal operation is to allow the SCOG26 to operate for its performance period of approximately an hour plus allow cool-down time prior to removal of the SCOG from the holding fixture and installation of a new SCOG26.

WSTF has performed previous testing of SCOG26 devices of nearly identical design to the SCOG26 device under investigation here. All previous SCOG26 test results indicate that normal operation is as described above.

The anomalous behavior that occurred within the compartment was as follows:

- The SCOG26 was ignited; and within an unknown number of seconds following ignition, an anomalous behavior began and continued to a catastrophic failure.
- Witnesses outside the compartment reported a loud "bang" or explosion emanating from within the compartment followed by large amounts of a whitish gas or vapor that filled nearby compartments.
- Nearby individuals described a chaotic event of smoke or vapor with debris and fragmentation of the container and nearby hardware.
- Reports indicated that several small fires, either of burning brick material or secondary fires, were seen immediately following the initial event.

4.2   Examination of Evidence

WSTF was provided with a sampling of post-event fragments from the SCOG26 canister and photographic images of the post-explosion effects to the compartment, along with other relevant information.

Post-event examination indicated large plastic deformation of several metallic support members of the SCOG rack assembly, and overall damage to the holder was significant. The bending magnitude and location is supporting evidence of a high-pressure region of gas that expanded in roughly a uniform manner from the SCOG26's failure location. The extent of damage indicated that immediate pressures at the SCOG surface could be in the range of several thousand pounds per square inch (PSI) at the moment of burst, concentrated within the upper portion of the vessel, based on the relative location of bending of the support structure and its assumed material strength. The anomalous rupture of the container suggests a reaction rate far in excess of normal operation, indicating the SCOG26 was generating gas at a rate exceeding the venting ability of the container, even with the two pressure relief devices and existing ports.

Nearby flat panels showed evidence of bending in a ductile manner, similar to metal panels exposed to incident overpressures on the order of 2 to 6 psi (13.8 to 41.4 kPa), at distances of ~ 3 to 6 ft (1 to 2 m) from the known location of the SCOG26. The large deformation without fracture of these panels indicates a relatively slow expansion rate or long loading time of milliseconds for the estimated pressure field. This differs for strong shock loads, seen in similar structures exposed to high explosive detonations, which typically see sub-millisecond loading times. Relative overpressures are assigned based on comparison to other explosive events effects (TM-1300 NAVPAC P-397 AFR 88-22, 1994).

Metal cabinets and lockers ~6 ft (2 m) or more from the event showed evidence of overpressures in the 1.0 to 4.0 psi (6.9 to 27.6 kPa) range, based on the amount of deflection and the exposed surface areas.

Nearly all glass panes on various gauges in the compartment failed (shattered), indicating nearly every surface in the compartment was exposed to incident overpressures of ~1.0 psi (6.9 kPa) or greater at some point during the event.

The overpressure estimates from surrounding equipment damage in the area suggest a time of loading and pressure magnitude in the compartment at levels known to be lethal or capable of severe injuries to exposed personnel (TM-1300 NAVPAC P-397 AFR 88-22, 1994).

The effects of pressure are often enhanced during reflection of the pressure waves, increasing the pressure an object is subjected to by up to 8 times the incident pressure in high explosive shocks, 2 to 6 times in low explosive events, and 2 to 3 times in pressurized gas vessel burst scenarios. Exact time of loading (duration) and magnitudes (pressure profile) can only be estimated from photographic evidence and material descriptions. However, the large deflections and lack of brisance[1] effects on nearby structures indicate pressure durations in the multi-millisecond range, suggesting a low explosive type event. High explosives tend to have short duration (sub-millisecond) high pressure loading profiles, often inducing brittle failures in nearby structures of the types present. No severe brittle behavior was evident in nearby structures.

Some evidence of strong reflected pressure pulses was provided by reports indicating objects traveling opposite (towards) the blast event location. This is typical when reflected pulses from walls or other objects have strong reflected pressure waves. The peak velocity of debris is often slower than the pressure pulse. Near reflecting surfaces, the pressure pulse will magnify and reflect back toward the debris. The debris can be subjected to greater force from the reflected pressure pulse and "reverse" its flight path. In some cases of centrally located explosions in interior spaces, the debris will "collect" near the point of explosion due to being pushed back to the epicenter from reflected pulses.

Photographic evidence also supports a relatively large thermal component in the surroundings, based on the degree of melting of some assumed plastic objects and visible traces of scorching. This presents a high probability of continued reaction of the SCOG26 material outside the container in a fine particulate or vapor phase combustion process, and may indicate the formation of a possible vapor cloud explosion (VCE) component in addition to the apparent mechanical or burst explosion of the SCOG26.

The canister remnants that were made available to WSTF for examination indicate a combination of both brittle and ductile failure in the 316 series stainless steel canister of the SCOG26, indicating a high strain rate event. This behavior is also seen in bursts of high-pressure gas storage vessels with thin-wall construction or large-scale oxidizer/fuel explosions. The container appeared to have more widespread brittle failure and smaller fragments near the top of the original container, close to the point of initial

---

[1] In addition to strength, explosive materials display a second characteristic, which is their shattering effect or brisance (from the French briser, to break), which is distinguished from their total work capacity. This characteristic is of practical importance in determining the effectiveness of an explosion in fragmenting shells, bomb casings, grenades, structures, and the like. The rapidity with which an explosive reaches its peak pressure is a measure of its brisance. (Wikipedia, 2008)

ignition. The section near the bottom of the container exhibited a more ductile response, and fragments were larger compared to those recovered from the top of the container. The failure point of the canister is most likely near the point where brittle fragments were generated. This region appears to be near the top section of the SCOG26, close to the point of initial ignition.

Curling of edges on the fragments was also noted. Curling of fracture edges is indicative of hot gases flowing past canister fragments and is typically found on thin fragments from casings surrounding explosives.

Evidence of a downward thrust on the support structure appeared directly below the canister location. This is another indication of a top-sided explosion of the canister, generating a rocketing effect of at least a portion of the SCOG26.

Fragment sizes ranged from relatively small fragments (less than 1 in. (2.54 cm) across) to larger specimens several inches in size. Full reconstruction of the canister was not possible from the limited number of fragments recovered, but evidence suggests a rapid increase in internal pressure due to an increased reaction rate between the oxidizer (sodium chlorate) and available fuel in a confined system well beyond what is deemed normal or nominal.

Typical high explosive events in thin-walled containers will shatter the container into many small fragments, leaving no larger sections. The presence of large fragments indicates an explosion of lower brisance than found in commercial high explosives. High explosives are not necessarily required to generate fragmentation of vessels. Both low explosives and high-pressure gas storage vessels can also generate brittle mode fragmentation in portions of the container material. The fragments formation is highly dependent on the rate the load is applied (strain rate), the pre-existing stress-strain state in the material, and the material properties. Low-explosive fragments are normally governed by the strain rate in the container wall during the deflagration event. Pressure vessels can have high strain induced by mechanical over-pressurization of the vessel or accidental exposure to excessive heat. Brittle behavior in gas storage vessels is most likely found near the point of failure with a transition to more ductile behavior at locations further from the failure point. Thin walled vessels tend to behave in a more brittle fashion than their thick-walled counterparts. In general, the faster the strain rate and the thinner the material the more likely brittle mode failure of the surrounding material will occur.

The primary fuels used in sodium chlorate based explosives are organic compounds (granulated sugars or hydrocarbons). The small grain size and intimate mixing of fuel and oxidizer allow the mixture to burn in a manner akin to black powder or smokeless powder, producing similar reaction rates and gas production rates. The burn rate is sufficient to raise the pressure in the vessel to several thousand pounds per square inch prior to rupture. This rapid increase in pressure develops high strain rates in the pipe wall, generating some fragmentation. The expanding hot products of combustion in chlorate-based explosives can then generate moderate overpressures of the type seen in other situations, based on similar rapid deflagration mechanisms.

The use of chlorate and perchlorate compounds mixed with oil falls under a class of explosive or energetic materials known as "Sprengel" explosives. A Sprengel explosive is any explosive compound made with a fuel and strong oxidizer, first invented by Herman Sprengel in the 1870s. These explosives can consist of nearly any fuel and oxidizer, but typically have one or both of the constituents in liquid form to enhance intimate contact between the fuel and oxidizer.

Chlorate-based explosive compounds exist, but the relative strength is highly dependent on the manner the fuel and oxidizer is mixed (degree of homogeneity) and particle size. Smaller particle sizes yield faster burn rates due to the increased surface area per unit mass. Liquid-liquid mixing is considered ideal when manufacturing a Sprengel explosive since this leads to a nearly homogeneous explosive mixture. Widespread use of chlorate-based explosives has become less commonplace in industrial applications, replaced by more efficient modern water gel based explosives, which provide the liquid-liquid mixing of the fuel and oxidizer. However, other solid-liquid Sprengel explosives such as ammonium nitrate and fuel oil (ANFO) are still used in large quantities in the mining industry.

4.2.1 Fragment Behavior

Fragmentation and gas expansion showed evidence that several metal "shards" of relatively small size (1 in. (2.54 cm) or less) had imbedded themselves at various points in surrounding material. These fragments were identified as coming from the original SCOG canister involved in the accident and not from failure of surrounding equipment. The penetration or imbedding of material indicated canister fragment velocities similar in nature to traditional ammunition ballistic ranges. Ballistic velocities in this range are ~ 1000 to 4000 ft/s (300 to 1200 m/s). These types of ballistic velocities are typical in low explosives or pressure vessel burst scenarios. For comparison a .22 caliber rifle slug exits at ~ 1000 ft/s (300 m/s), and a high power rifle (e.g., .30-06) travels in excess of 3000 ft/s (920 m/s). Multiple fragments from an explosion typically form a Gaussian velocity distribution; however, there are not enough data to make a determination of the average velocity of all fragments from the available photos. It is estimated the fragments were on the lower end of the ballistic range provided (~ 1,000 ft/s, ~ 300 m/s), indicating the fragments were most likely driven by a low explosive event.

High explosives generate different ballistic effects from fragmenting casings. The peak velocities in high explosive generated fragments can approach the detonation velocity of the explosive. Detonation velocities in typical high explosives are on the order of 19,700 to 26,250 ft/s (6 to 8 km/s) (Gibbs and Popolato, 1980). Fragments of these velocities are in the hypervelocity regime (> 3 km/s) and generate different impact characteristics from ballistic impacts. Typical hypervelocity impacts will generate sufficient heat and pressure to make both the projectile and surface of impact behave as fluids, leaving impact craters with similar aspect ratios of depth and diameter as other impact crater formation mechanisms found in nature (e.g., the surface of the moon). There were no reports or indications found of crater formation in the area of the event. This further indicates the fragments were most likely driven by a low explosive event.

4.2.2 General Accident Conclusions

The conclusion from the evidence is that an explosion or explosions occurred during the failure of the SCOG26 resulting in heat, blast, and fragmentation effects within a confined space. The overpressures and mechanical deformation of structures suggest a moderate pressure level and long-duration blast loading (multi-millisecond). The behavior and observations suggest a low-explosive event and not a high-explosive detonation capable of higher pressures of shorter duration. Lack of cratering and evidence of fragment imbedding indicate fragment velocities on the order of high sonic or low supersonic speeds similar to those found in low explosive or mechanical pressure vessel burst events. Evidence of a possible secondary reaction was found in the photographic evidence. This suggests the probability that a secondary vapor phase reaction occurred, generating an extensive thermal load on surrounding objects out to several feet from the SCOG26. This secondary reaction occurred primarily outside the confinement of the SCOG26.

4.3   Fault Tree, Root Cause, and Failure Modes and Effects Analysis

Three different analytical techniques were used to analyze the accident, document lines of reasoning, and guide the experimental process. Each of the three techniques serves a useful purpose. None of the three techniques alone can fully capture the analysis. The three analytical techniques are: fault tree analysis, root cause analysis, and failure modes and effects analysis (FMEA).

4.3.1   Fault Tree Analysis

The first analytical technique used was a fault tree analysis. The results of a brainstorming session conducted at WSTF in July 2007 were transcribed into a fault tree by personnel in the International Space Station (ISS) Safety Office. The fault tree does an excellent job documenting the lines of reasoning that were raised in the brainstorming session, studied analytically, and dismissed by analysis. NASA needs to document the lines of reasoning that were analytically dismissed. The fault tree, shown in Figure 3, documents the process of analysis that focused experimental work on liquid organic contamination, chemical briquette fracture, and physical constraint, and dismissed all other potential factors.

Some notes on the dismissed possibilities are listed as follows:

- Contamination with water cannot explain the evidence. The latent heat of phase change for water is too great, and there is no mechanism of steam formation that would trigger a runaway reaction rate.
- Contamination with a volatile organic contaminant in vapor phase cannot explain the evidence. There is not enough volume inside the canister to provide enough mass for a volatile contaminant to have sufficient energy.
- Contamination with a solid organic contaminant cannot explain the evidence. There is no credible mechanism for solid phase organic material to be mixed inside and distributed within the chemical briquette without being noticed during lot acceptance testing. Any solid contaminant located inside the canister but outside the chemical briquette would burn like an oxygen-enhanced fire rather than explode.
- Iron enrichment cannot explain the evidence. Iron consumes oxygen and releases heat, and in extreme cases where the iron and the chlorate are mixed at stoichiometric ratios, a very large amount of heat would be produced, but no gas. Local "hot spots" of iron-rich portions of the briquette have been shown to produce enough heat to melt through the metal housing of the canister and cause the canister to burn through, but iron enrichment should not cause an explosion.
- A failure of the percussive cap cannot explain the evidence. There is not enough mass in the percussive cap to generate enough energy.
- No missing or extra components can explain the evidence. Specifically, an enlarged or iron-rich booster section cannot explain the evidence. The booster section produces additional heat, but it consumes gaseous oxygen.
- Physical blockage of the vent holes cannot explain the evidence. There is no credible mechanism to block all of the vents and both relief valves. Reports of loud hissing indicate that gas was exiting through the vent holes.

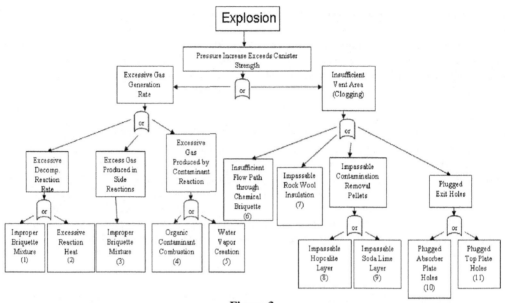

Figure 3
Fault Tree

4.3.2   Root Cause Analysis

Root cause analysis does not document the possibilities that were considered and dismissed. Instead, it focuses on describing one event (the accident being analyzed) and then identifies all contributing causes. Root cause analysis involves a forward looking cause-to-effect audit, and a backward looking effect-to-cause audit. The cause-to-effect audit is especially helpful. Root cause analysis requires the analyst to ask the question, "If these causes occur, does the described effect occur 100 percent of the time?" If the answer is "sometimes" instead of "100 percent of the time," more causes need to be identified. There is a chronological mapping of cause and effect; the cause always happens before the effect.

A root cause analysis of the incident was performed. The analysis is described as follows, using an analysis that is only one tier deep.

Effect: SCOG26 Explosion

Causes: 1)   SCOG26 being initiated
          2)   SCOG26 in SCOG holder
          3)   SCOG26 is fractured
          4)   SCOG26 fracture is undetected
          5)   SCOG26 briquette contaminated with liquid organic contaminant
          6)   Contamination not detected

4.3.3   Failure Modes and Effects Analysis

Failure modes and effects analyses are comprehensive analyses of an entire system. FMEAs do not focus on a single mishap; instead they try to consider all of the possible hazards in a design. Nevertheless, some notes about possible hazards were taken that should be formally documented. Contributing notes to an FMEA of the SCOG26 system include:

- Iron rich "hot spots" can lead to burn-through events.
- Chemicals in the percussive igniter can react with the SCOG26 to form trace amounts of mixed oxides of nitrogen (NOx).
- Improper labeling of lot and batch number can hamper configuration management and make lot and batch identification and recall difficult.
- Contamination with water can cause candles to fail to ignite.
- Chlorate chemical contaminated with liquid organic is shock sensitive when the mixture is nearly homogeneous and at or near stoichiometry.
- Insufficient lot testing can lead to unidentified manufacturing defects.

4.4   Numerical Simulation and Energy Estimations

The probability of hydrocarbon contamination was investigated by using chemical analysis on fragments of the SCOG26 recovered at the accident site. The first step in the analysis was to determine which type of fuel is most likely to have been introduced into the normally fuel-lean mixture of the SCOG26.

Analysis using both Scanning Electron Microscopy/Energy dispersive X-ray spectroscopy (SEM/EDS) and Fourier Transform Infrared (FT-IR) Spectroscopy showed unusually high levels of carbon and carbon-based compounds on the fragment samples, including hydrocarbons. Further examination showed a liquid aliphatic hydrocarbon compound (C_nH_{2n+2}) is present on fragments recovered from the accident. These compounds were found both on the interior and exterior surfaces of the fragments. Some fragments were found to have carbonaceous residue on the interior surfaces, indicating combustion of hydrocarbon compounds was probable. The carbon was not deemed to be from the carbon contained in 316 series stainless steel (the material of the canister). The candle brick material itself contains no carbon.

The available information led to hydrocarbon oil being the most probable source of fuel within the container. The exact composition of the hydrocarbon oil was unknown. The properties are similar to a multitude of hydraulic, lubricating, or mineral oils, of which several candidate types were known to exist in the proximity of the SCOG26 prior to the energetic event.

Additional evidence pointed to possible seal integrity issues in post-accident studies of remaining SCOG26 canisters. Seal failure or complete removal of the protective cap allows paths for the introduction of hydrocarbon fluids into the canister during handling or storage. Alternate paths can also occur from openings formed in the SCOG26 container from corrosion or rough handling, allowing seepage through seams or splits.

The first task was to determine the theoretical amount of heat energy that introduction of oil into the candle brick material would achieve provided the complete combustion of the oil with the iron and sodium chlorate mixture. The method used was to simulate combustion of the oil and SCOG26 material using the Chemical Equilibrium with Applications (CEA) computer code developed at NASA Glenn Research Center for solving similar problems of fuel and oxidizer reactions using equilibrium states to define thermodynamic properties and products of reaction (Gordon and McBride, 1994).

The problem was reduced to find a maximum heat output of a mixture of the primary components of the candle brick material with the addition of an aliphatic hydrocarbon oil to reach a near stoichiometric condition between the sodium chlorate oxidizer, the iron fuel, and a suspected hydrocarbon.

Examination of the apparent density of the brick material compared to the maximum theoretical density of the constituents indicated the void volume in the brick material was ~ 25 percent. Coincidentally, a void space of 25 percent by volume in the brick material allows space for oil to be absorbed and dispersed throughout the material at near stoichiometric concentrations, or 10 percent by mass. This dispersion into the void spaces provides a degree of "mixing" of the oxidizer and fuel while forming a heterogeneous compound.

The particular hydrocarbon compound used in the numerical simulation was oil consisting of tetradecane ($C_{14}C_{30}$) as the sole contaminant, used to find the approximate heat of combustion starting at 1 atmosphere (101 kPa) and 300 K (77 °F (25 °C)).

The primary results are the equilibrium conditions of the flame (adiabatic flame temperature for the mixture) and the heat produced on a kJ/kg basis. The model used 1 mole of iron, 10 moles of $NaClO_3$, and 0.566 moles of $C_{14}H_{30}$ to represent the mixture expected if the void spaces in the brick material are saturated.

The heat of combustion is found by solving the system at the adiabatic burn conditions including the phase changes of the fuels and oxidizers, and comparing it to a burn that occurs with heat transfer to maintain room temperatures. The difference in bulk enthalpy at the two states provides the amount of heat removal required to maintain the fixed temperature boundary condition compared to the adiabatic case. This difference yields the heat of combustion and accounts for phase changes within the process.

The primary results indicated a maximum heat of combustion of ~ 5,375 kJ/kg and an adiabatic flame temperature of 2537 K when burned at 1 atmosphere pressure (14.7 psi, 101 kPa). Typically, real reactions can never achieve the maximum theoretical temperatures predicted by the CEA program; however, the solution does give the ideal limiting value. The results identified combustion products consisting of 24 different species of carbon, sodium, oxygen, chlorine, hydrogen; iron compounds were likely present in the flame, with the bulk of the products being H_2O, CO_2, O_2, and NaCl in the gaseous state along with monatomic oxygen. A form of iron oxide is also formed at these temperatures, but remains a liquid at the flame temperature at 1 atmosphere. The species in the flame will recombine to form a lower number of stable species at room temperature. Combustion is a complex process, and numerical tools are limited by the assumptions made. In general, the solutions agree well when compared to experimental values, but are not exact.

The amount of heat energy is considerable due to the oil addition, and this combination exceeds the 4184 kJ/kg stored chemical energy of trinitrotoluene (TNT). The ideal mixing of oil and metal as fuels with sodium chlorate material can produce the amounts of heat energy comparable to other pyrotechnics, rocket fuels based on chlorates and metals, or other low or high explosives. The difference between the energetic materials lies in the manner or method of energy release to provide classifications between fuels, propellants, and explosives of equal chemical energy. The conclusion is oxygen candles with oil added in stoichiometric amounts can be classified as an energetic material. Determination of the rate of release will determine the class of energetic material.

Historically, chlorate-based energetic materials near stoichiometry are used as solid propellants with combustion rates far below those found in high explosives. The material formed from the candle and oil is expected to be similar and act as a propellant or gunpowder-like substance. High order detonation, even under confinement, is unlikely. However, a confined rapid increase in burn rate is expected to produce large quantities of gas leading to a mechanical over-pressurization failure of the container, creating an explosion. This is not a true detonation as seen in high explosives. High explosives can generate large quantities of gas and strong overpressures without the aid of confinement. Low-explosive and pyrotechnic types of materials, when unconfined, typically "burn" or deflagrate but do not "mass detonate."

The most likely scenario is a sub-sonic burn or deflagration within a confined environment with insufficient venting of combustion products to avert a primary mechanical explosion. Large quantities of gas can be produced in relatively short time frames; and these gases can expand rapidly, producing damaging overpressures and fragmentation of the container as is often seen in similar situations.

4.4.1 Gas Buildup Approximation Summary

Normally a SCOG26 will produce 2600 L (92 scf) of gas at STP in ~60 min from a mass of brick material of 10.2 kg (22.5 lb), based on product literature and previous testing of similar SCOG26 devices at WSTF. This provides a gas generation rate of up to a maximum normal rate of 1 L (0.035 cf) of gaseous oxygen per second (at STP), with the remaining oxygen combining with the iron to form iron oxide compounds and the chlorate-producing sodium chloride (NaCl, "table salt").

The approximation presented here assumes the gas void volume in the container, which includes the insulation and gas paths, is ~ 1 L. If this is true, then a completely sealed container, if allowed to cool back to standard temperature after combustion completes, would have 2600 L of gas compressed into a 1-L volume. The pressure would then be on the order of 2600 atmospheres (38, 000 psi), assuming near ideal gas behavior. However, the reaction occurs at temperatures in excess of 300 °C (573 K, 572 °F) and approaches 400. °C (673 K, 752 °F). This temperature is more than two times the standard atmospheric temperature of 298 K (77 °F (25 °C)). Thus the pressure at end of combustion would be closer to 5200+ atmospheres (76,000+ psi) prior to cooling in a closed system. Conclusion: When confined, the brick material itself produces significant amounts of gas and would burst a completely closed vessel within minutes.

The next case is to compare the gas output from a SCOG26 at near stoichiometric conditions with oil. The oil is assumed to be $C_{14}H_{30}$ (tetradecane). This will ideally burn with the available gaseous oxygen, as shown in Eq. 2:

$$C_{14}H_{30} + 21.5\ O_2 = 15\ H_2O + 14\ CO_2 \qquad (2)$$

Thus for every 21.5 moles of oxygen generated, the oil will "convert" the oxygen to steam and carbon dioxide having a total number of moles of 29. This means that the pressure component from the oil combustion with oxygen will generate 1.34 times the moles of a "normal" SCOG26 reaction. This ratio remains nearly constant for a range of hydrocarbons, since smaller or larger hydrocarbon chains will balance on a mass/mole basis. However, the final pressure is not 1.34 times the pressure of the "normal" combustion discussed previously. The end temperature will be increased due to the combustive energy released from the oil. The adiabatic flame temperature of oil, iron, and sodium chlorate at stoichiometry is calculated from computer models to be ~ 2570 K if burned at a constant pressure of one standard atmosphere. The temperature of combustion in a closed volume will be higher and is assumed here for illustration to be on the order of 3000 K (10 times standard temperature) as a rough approximation. The molar balance yields a closed pressure having 1.34 times the moles normally present, but now the temperature is nearly 5 times higher than the nominal decomposition/combustion process (573 K). If the closed volume is allowed to cool back to 300 K, the pressure would be ~ 3,500 atmospheres (51,500 psi). But at 10 times the temperature, the pressure would increase to ~ 35,000 atmospheres (5×10^5 psi). This example is only illustrative and is based on the assumption there is no heat loss in an enclosed volume and all the products remain gaseous from oil combustion alone. The real system has another component that cannot be ignored, which is the sodium chloride (NaCl) formed after oxygen is liberated from the sodium chlorate.

The candle under normal operating conditions creates molten salt that will instantly "freeze" at typical operating temperature, providing no pressure component is in the system. The boiling point at 1 atmosphere of sodium chloride is 1465 °C (1738 K, 2669 °F). The relatively high flame temperature from oil combustion can begin to vaporize sodium chloride to add an additional component to the pressure. The ratio of sodium chloride to the initial release of O_2 from $NaClO_3$ is 2/3, since two sodium chlorate molecules yield two sodium chloride and three oxygen molecules. Thus there is an additional 14.3 moles of salt vapor added per 29 moles of steam and carbon dioxide generated under ideal conditions. This increases the total moles of products by ~ 50 percent. This is unrealistic, since extreme pressures in an enclosed volume combustion process will force some of the heavier compounds back into a liquid state. The probability of liquid products or reactants under pressure at or above their standard atmospheric boiling temperature adds a degree of complexity to the actual burst event and is summarized below.

The above illustrative values are provided to show that, when oil is added to the candle, the reaction will produce more gas than a nominal SCOG26 reaction and generate not only steam and CO_2, but also sodium chloride gas at elevated temperatures and pressures. However, there is an added complication of the surrounding material. Some of the heat of reaction can begin to melt or vaporize unreacted sodium chloride and oil to produce more intimate mixing prior to combustion. This can cause an increase in reaction rate, accelerating the combustion process. This also poses a problem if the container bursts while molten or vaporous sodium chlorate is present along with unreacted oil. The vessel will contain, just prior to burst, superheated fluids well above their typical boiling points at 1 atmosphere.

The dynamics of a bursting vessel introduce an interesting problem for determining the overpressure expected. During the rapid buildup of pressure in the container, the sodium chloride's temperature may increase to well above its typical boiling point at 1 atmosphere but be forced to remain in liquid form at high pressure. This may also be true for the water generated from combustion and the sodium chlorate in the system, as well as the suspected oil contaminant. Once the canister ruptures and the hot gaseous products escape, the canister may still contain liquid reactants and products that are gases at atmospheric pressure at the reaction temperature. The sudden drop in pressure begins a second process with potentially greater catastrophic effects than the initial release of hot gases (the mechanical burst event). The molten salt, water, sodium chlorate, and oil may "flash" to vapor form, creating a partial or full boiling liquid expanding vapor explosion (BLEVE) effect.

A BLEVE can generate a second overpressure that occurs within the vessel and is often stronger than the initial burst overpressure. This secondary explosion origin is within the container and can induce high strain rate behavior in the container material, causing brittle failure or enhance the ductile failure rate of the container walls. The BLEVE reaction itself can be partially surrounded by solid material in the case of the SCOG26. The rapid formation of gas can also shatter and eject the contents of the container, causing a debris cloud to form outside the vessel of unreacted brick material.

The main difference between a SCOG26 and classical BLEVE behavior is that the heat source in the SCOG26 is generated within the container, while typical BLEVE scenarios use external heating.

The field of study of molten salt or sodium chlorate BLEVE is essentially nonexistent, since most molten processes with these substances are not typically conducted in high-pressure vessels and are difficult to generate experimentally. However, any substance that is liquefied by pressure at high temperature can support a BLEVE under certain conditions.

The mechanical explosion and possible BLEVE behavior during a SCOG26 failure scenario can generate a cloud of either vapor directly from the BLEVE or a cloud of fine particles of unreacted brick material. The cloud may still contain fuel and has a high probability of having excess oxidizer present. The vapor cloud or particulate cloud can form a third explosive mechanism, for example, a vapor, dust cloud explosion, termed a *thermobaric* event.

Rapidly burning fuel and oxidizer within the cloud can generate both significant overpressures within a volume, and a "fireball" with temperatures in excess of 2000 K throughout the reaction zone. This reaction zone can encompass large volumes prior to completion causing both thermal (*thermo*) and pressure (*baric*) effects, often with catastrophic outcomes.

Numerical and analytical results indicate that the addition of oil into the system can generate significant heat and increase pressure not only within but also outside the container, depending on the process. The key parameter in the failure mode of the canister is the initial reaction rate. If the reaction proceeds slowly enough, the vessel can vent the pressure without structural failure. However, the faster the reaction, the greater is the pressurization rate. The pressurization rate can exceed the venting ability of the container and pressure relief devices, leading to a mechanical explosion of the contained gases. The products of combustion along with oxidizer and fuel may also be forced into a pressure and temperature region where some of the products and reactants remain liquid even at the elevated temperature prior to vessel failure. Upon rupture a BLEVE can occur, leading to a secondary blast stronger than the initial canister burst pressure. This can then be followed by a third energetic event similar to a thermobaric device if sufficient fuel and oxidizer remain in the expanding vapor or dust cloud, which itself ignites and deflagrates. A BLEVE is a mechanical expansion and not a detonation. The energetic material itself is considered a low explosive and may deflagrate, but does not truly detonate.

Several factors must occur simultaneously, including proper fuel/oxidizer ratios and surface area, to provide the environment for a rapid reaction to begin the process of catastrophic failure. The ideal reaction energetic release potential is considerable, based on chemical stored energy and the confinement of the canister.

The system itself is capable of complex behavior in the manner in which energy is released, making the task of isolating the exact sequence of events difficult. The evidence supports rapid combustion leading to canister failure. It is unknown if the degree of fragmentation in the original accident was from high stress rates produced in the material from the rapid internal pressure rise alone, or if the initial pressure release prompted a BLEVE-like explosion leading to enhanced fragmentation.

The probability of an ignitable vapor or dust cloud and continued burning of material in a fireball is supported from photographic evidence of the accident location, showing thermal damage to various surfaces and components several feet from the failed SCOG26 location. This fireball could be either a "slow" thermal chemical reaction (deflagration) or, under ideal conditions, transition to a fuel and oxidizer detonation. Regardless of deflagration or detonation behavior in the cloud, a strong overpressure can be produced. The vapor or dust cloud explosion typically produce lower peak pressures than high explosives, but the slow reaction rate compared to high explosives typically generates longer-duration pressure pulses. The final complication is if a cloud is formed the exact ignition point could be anywhere within the cloud perimeter, making the center of expansion nearly impossible to predict.

The situation and circumstance show that the addition of fuel to the system can produce a variety of effects depending on timing, mixtures, and environmental variables. This system is particularly hazardous, since up to three sources of blast and two combustion modes can be generated in a short time span. Any object in close proximity can experience damaging overpressures and reflected pressures decreasing in severity with distance from the source. A severe thermal hazard with momentary exposure to temperatures above 2000 K is a definite probability in the event of vapor or dust cloud formation with subsequent ignition.

4.4.2 Oil Mass Estimates for Accident Scenario

This is the most difficult parameter to determine, since there are so many factors involved in creating an energetic material. Energy comparisons alone are typically not an adequate measurement when comparing energetic materials of different classes (e.g., high explosives vs. low explosives vs. propellants vs. fuels); thus it is inappropriate to assign a direct TNT equivalence to a mechanical burst, BLEVE, or VCE, due to differences in peak pressures and time of loading for comparable total energies.

A parametric estimate is provided here to illustrate the amount of energetic material that can be formed given a fixed amount of oil. The amount of oxidizer in the canister allows up to ~ 1300 mL (46 fluid oz) to be added to reach near stoichiometric conditions if all the oil is absorbed and is evenly distributed in the roughly 25 percent void space of the brick material. An example case is provided below for 100 mL of oil (3.4 oz) to obtain the amount of ideal stoichiometric energetic material that can be formed.

100 mL (3.4 oz) of hydrocarbon oil of specific gravity 0.72 has a mass of ~ 72 g (0.159 lb). This can convert ~ 1/13 (7.7 percent) of the total brick mass into an ideal energetic material near stoichiometry. The total "dry" brick mass of 1/13 of the brick is 0.784 kg (1.73 lb) and, combined with oil, will create 0.856 kg (1.89 lb) of energetic material. In general, each unit mass of oil can make ~ 11 unit masses of energetic material for the SCOG26 case.

The type and extent of damage seen during the accident can only be crudely bounded and compared to low explosives devices, BLEVE, or VCE events. The reaction certainly involved more than gram quantities of material.

The material in brick form has limited surface area and, when oil-enriched, can burn like solid rocket propellant. If the surface area is increased considerably (ground or powdered), then the reaction rate can be increased to mimic other powdered propellants such as gunpowder or smokeless powder. Even moderate cracking to form large chunks of material can increase the available surface area several times above a pristine candle. The behavior of the SCOG26 does not depend completely on the amount of energetic material but also on the rate of combustion, governed primarily by available surface area.

The rate of combustion also depends on the degree of confinement (pressure of burn). In the accident scenario, the rate of combustion is a function of an ever-increasing pressure profile until structural failure occurs. This allows the reaction to start slowly and accelerate as pressure builds. The SCOG26 does have some means of pressure relief; but choked flow can occur, effectively limiting the ability of the container to control the pressure. This behavior is controlled in rocket motors by means of allowing supersonic flow from the combustion chamber, establishing a steady state balance between chamber pressure, surface area, rate of combustion, and temperature. If this were not the case, rocket motors can fail in a similar manner as the SCOG26 due to rapid increases in pressure. The SCOG26 relief devices only allow flow that is sonically limited by orifice type structures, effectively limiting the escape velocity of gases. This leads to a rapid pressurization and explosion, provided gas production continues within the canister at increasing rates.

The limiting factors in the magnitude of a SCOG26 explosion include the amount of fuel, surface area, and degree of confinement of the SCOG26 in question. The probability is high that all three possible explosion modes (mechanical, BLEVE, VCE) contributed to the overall observed effects found at the accident scene.

The hypothesis presented thus far needed to be verified. A test program was developed to examine the behavior of SCOG26 devices when subjected to varying amounts of hydrocarbon contamination. These tests performed are the subject of the following sections.

4.5   Small Scale Testing Summary

A portion of the testing was conducted on the brick material itself to determine if hydrocarbon oil contamination posed an immediate safety threat, due to either spontaneous reaction or increased sensitivity. These tests were conducted to ensure that large scale testing could be conducted in a safe manner and to characterize possible mechanisms leading to the observed explosion effects.

A brief review of those results is presented here including:

- Normal brick material unconfined burn
- Oil-doped sample reactivity and combustion testing
- High surface area oil-doped impact sensitivity testing
- Liquid hydrocarbon absorption rate

4.5.1   Normal Brick Material Unconfined Burn

Samples of pristine candle material were sectioned from a SCOG26 brick. These samples were exposed to direct heating via the use of a nickel chromium resistive heating element capable of producing temperature well in excess of the ignition point of iron and sodium chlorate mixtures.

The finding was as follows: Unconfined sodium chlorate brick material can ignite under direct heat application; however, once the heat source is removed, the fuel-lean material is incapable of continued combustion and self-extinguishes at an ambient pressure of 12.5 psia or 86.2 kPa (WSTF ambient) and room temperature for samples of the size used. It is theorized that the brick material outside of the container does not have the aid of the container's ability to maintain a thermal environment, greater than 300 °C (572 °F), capable of continuous sodium chlorate decomposition. Without the benefit of an insulated environment, the material is intrinsically safe for handling in small scale quantities with respect to accidental ignition due to its self-extinguishing properties in a laboratory environment. An example of the unconfined burn test is shown in Figure 4. The sample is 1 in. (2.54 cm) wide. It cannot be concluded that larger pieces with large surface area are incapable of maintaining decomposition and combustion external to the container without further testing.

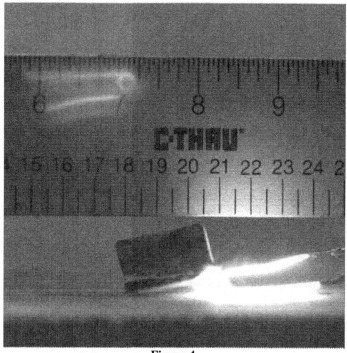

Figure 4
Unconfined Ignition Attempt using a Nickel-Chromium Hot Wire Ignition Source

4.5.2   Oil-doped Sample Reactivity and Combustion Testing

The oil selected for use in testing is aliphatic hydrocarbon petroleum-based hydraulic oil manufactured by Coilhose Pneumatics, Inc. (CAS# 64742-58-1 and 64742-62-7). This type of lightweight oil was selected to facilitate absorption of the oil into the porous brick material with an even dispersion.

No immediate reaction was observed upon addition of the oil, and the combination was stable at room temperature.

The samples were exposed to a high-temperature heat source (hotwire) and combustion did occur. The behavior in an unconfined environment was similar to an oil-based candle, allowing continued combustion of the oil while decomposition of the brick material provided additional oxygen to promote combustion. Once the oil was consumed the remaining brick material self extinguished in all tests.

The screening test performed here was not time–based, and the true burning rate was not measured. The sample burned with the intensity of an oil candle or alcohol lamp, producing laminar flames of ~1 in. (2.54 cm) in length. No violent reaction was noted; however, the oil impregnated regions were consumed in a matter of seconds indicating accelerated combustion compared to uncontaminated samples. There was some indication of yellow flames, possibly indicating some sodium in the flame; however, the spectrum was not analyzed for elements or compounds. An example of the oil-doped ignition test in a laboratory setting is shown in Figure 5.

17

Figure 5
Brick Material with Oil Burn Test

4.5.3 High Surface Area Oil-Doped Impact Sensitivity Testing

A test series was performed on the material to gauge the impact sensitivity of the material when in powder form. Samples of the brick material were ground in a standard mortar-pestle to the consistency of refined sugar. This greatly increases the surface area of the material and allows for a higher degree of homogeneity when using oil in the mixture. No spontaneous reaction occurred.

The candle material itself is calculated to have an approximate void volume of 25 percent based on the density of the brick compounds versus the uncrushed brick material density. Coincidentally, this amount of void space is nearly ideal for obtaining a near stoichiometric ratio between oil and brick material.

The oil-doped samples were prepared with a near stoichiometric mixture of oil. This occurs at roughly 10 percent oil by mass when combined with the brick material and offers the greatest likelihood for reaction.

Two test series were performed in a standard drop weight test machine to measure if a sudden input at several known energy levels would generate a reaction. The test is performed by placing a sample in a small cup and the striker plug located in contact with the material, forming partial confinement. A drop weight is raised on a rail system to a known height and released. The weight impacts the striker plug and reactions are noted. This was a screening test for reactivity, and qualitative data were gathered on a "reaction"/"no reaction" basis and the type of reaction was noted. Each test was repeated several times to generate statistically relevant threshold values for reaction, to gauge the sensitivity of material in question.

Primary Results:

The pristine candle material showed "no reaction" at all settings of input energy available.

The oil-doped samples showed "reaction" at all input levels down to the lowest setting of the machine of 10 ft-lb (13.6 J) energy input. The reaction was noted to be a "pop" or "bang," indicating a rapid high-speed combustion (deflagration) of the material occurred. This was a relatively simple screening test, but several items were learned from the testing.

1. Compression heating at energy levels of 10 ft-lb of finely powdered material was sufficient to cause a deflagration of the sample in the cup configuration. No lower limit was established.
2. The metallic sample cup did not sustain significant damage, indicating low probability of a detonation.
3. Reaction rates were accelerated by confinement, increase in surface area, and pressure. (It is noted here that this behavior is typical of most energetic materials.)

4.5.4 Liquid Hydrocarbon Absorption Rate

The testing of small samples concluded with a test of vertical absorption of oil. This was done to examine the effects of placing the material in a pool of oil and recording the travel of oil through the material by means of visual indicators. The brick material changes appearance and becomes darker when saturated with oil. This allowed the tracking of oil progressing upward through the material over time. The 1.5 in. (3.8 cm) tall sample shown in Figure 6 shows the progression of the oil over a 6-h period. This illustrates that oil can readily be absorbed into the material over time via capillary action.

Therefore, once a liquid hydrocarbon is present within the canister, the oil should readily diffuse into the material within a few hours of exposure. Actual diffusion rates within the canister were not measured.

4.6   Introduction to Large Scale Testing

The lessons learned from the small scale testing and other analysis provided the baseline information of large scale testing. The intent of the large scale testing was to understand the factors that could lead to a catastrophic failure as found in the original accident. The next section is devoted to detailing these attempts and the reactions observed.

Figure 6
Oil Soak Absorption Test (6 h Total)

5.0 Large Scale Testing

The small scale testing, examination of forensic evidence, and fault tree analysis indicated a high probability that the anomalous behavior of the SCOG26 device in question was due to the accidental introduction of a foreign fuel to the candle, the highest probability of which would be a hydrocarbon based fluid. This changed the candle behavior from a slow burning self-sustaining reaction and decomposition of sodium chlorate to liberate oxygen, to a higher speed reaction generating primarily oxygen, carbon dioxide, steam, and sodium chloride vapor that overpressurized the container.

The next step in the investigation was to examine the behavior of actual SCOG26 canisters and determine the effects of adding the assumed hydrocarbon contamination. It was established from analysis and small scale testing that the candles can be transformed from a relatively benign oxygen generating system to a potentially large-scale low explosive by the addition of oil to near stoichiometric levels, increasing the homogeneity of the mixture, and increasing the surface area for combustion (granulation or cracks). The stoichiometry values suggest that the addition of ~ 10 percent by mass of oil mixed with the chlorate-iron candle material can have a significant chemical-stored energy on par with other low and high explosive chemical compounds.

Historically, chlorates or other strong oxidizers have been used to manufacture a class of fuel and oxidizer bi-component explosives or Sprengel-type explosives. The most common of these in widespread use today is ammonium nitrate and fuel oil (ANFO). Granulated chlorates are often used in the manufacture of low explosives or propellant like mixtures with solid organic fuels such as sugar or with liquid fuels like oil. However, the candle material differs in the ability to achieve an effective "mixture" while in brick form. The voids of the candle material leave finite-size pockets of oil surrounded by candle material. The compartmentalization of fuel tends to limit the linear burn rate of the material and moderate the speed of combustion since it is a non-homogenous mixture.

The explosion mechanics is controlled by three primary factors. The first factor is the pressure in the system. The higher the pressure the faster the linear burn rate becomes. The second factor is surface area. The more surface area for reaction, the faster the overall volumetric burn rate becomes, even at a steady linear burn rate of the bulk material. The last factor is the hardest to quantify but deals with the strength of the container itself. The pressure increases the burn rate, but eventually the container will fail. The rate of pressure buildup and final burst pressure directly relates to the energy release from the primary mechanical explosion of compressed gas at time of burst. This is to say, the stronger the container the more violent the eventual mechanical explosion can become.

Local contributing factors will also affect the explosive behavior. These include the proximity to ideal stoichiometric conditions, the degree of homogeneity of the mixture, and concentration gradients.

The large scale testing described in the following section details the step-by-step approach in recreating not only the estimated energy output of the system, but also an attempt to bound the required reaction rate to cause a catastrophic failure with pressure relief devices present to recreate the accident conditions.

The recreation of the conditions in the accident scenario is based on the addition of a known quantity of hydrocarbon fluid into the test specimen (a SCOG26). The tests were conducted at WSTF's remote blast facility specifically designed to study explosions within the range of energy output expected from these tests. The tests used "new" SCOG26 canisters of the same design and specifications as the SCOG26 involved in the accident. Each test used one SCOG26 (test article) per test. The test series progressed as follows: free-standing testing of SCOG26 with oil; testing of SCOG26s that are damaged or cracked to increase internal surface area; and testing of SCOG26s in holders that partially constrain the canister in a manner similar to the accident. The last two tests used standard SCOG26 holder assemblies identical to the one used in the accident.

The system used was constructed to allow remote introduction of oil into the test article prior to initial activation. This was later changed to a manual addition method once procedures were perfected. Activation used the standard .410 igniter cartridge specifically designed for this type of SCOG26. Activation was conducted remotely using a solenoid driven plunger and striker pin assembly to simulate the normal manual ignition operation.

Primary Test Apparatus:

The primary test system is located on the WSTF 300-ft (92-m) diameter blast pad. The test article was situated at the center of the pad along with blast mitigation protection for instrumentation and a witness plate barricade to limit travel of fragments while providing near field penetration and damage data in a semi-confined space similar to the accident location. The location of the test was designated as "ground zero". Operations were conducted by trained ordnance personnel, and command and control were provided by a single individual designated as the Test Conductor (TC). Control and instrumentation for the test was provided via command lines to a hardened control room 500 ft (153 m) from ground zero. Pad operations were monitored via closed circuit camera within the access-controlled 700 Area at WSTF.

Primary test data were obtained via high speed Phantom[1] digital video cameras and standard speed video, audio, and thermocouple data.

Initial blast mitigation to contain debris was provided by a Lexan[2] steel frame and earth support structure designed to moderate maximum theoretical explosive yields but not completely contain an event. Later testing substituted a plywood structure for the Lexan walls in the blast mitigation and witness plate dual-role barrier.

Initial oil addition was test specific. Tests 1, 2 and 3 used a remote operated system. Later tests opted for a manual approach.

General test setup was as follows:

- Place SCOG26 in position
- Remove sealing lid
- Induce damage (if required by test)
- Attach instrumentation (thermocouples)
- Add predetermined oil amount (method is test specific)
- Allow diffusion of oil into brick material (test specific)
- Remotely trigger igniter
- Observe and record results

The following sections detail each test, based on the test matrix shown in Table 1.

---

[1] Phantom® is a registered trademark of Vision Research, Inc., Wayne, New Jersey.
[2] Lexan® is a registered trademark of General Electric Company, Schenectady, New York

Table 1
Test Matrix

Test Designator	Test Type	Contaminant Oil[a] (mL)	Condition	Radiograph Serial Number	Soak Time	Oil Introduction Path
COGA1	Raw Candle	400	New	n/a	24 h	Top Surface
COGA2	Oil – Filter – Pristine	400	New	n/a	3 h	Through Filter
COGA3	Oil – Filter – Pristine	600	Induced Cracking	n/a	4 days	Through Filter
COGA4	Oil – Direct – Flawed	100	Induced Cracking	003	5 days	Direct Through Port
COGA5	Oil –Direct - Flawed	100	Induced Cracking	002	5 days	Direct Through Port
COGA6	Oil –Direct – Pristine	100	New	n/a	5 days	Direct Through Port
COGA7	Oil –Direct – Flawed	25	Induced Cracking	001	5 days	Direct Through Port
COGA8	Oil –Direct – Flawed	100	Induced Cracking	004	5 days	Direct Through Port
COGA9	Oil –Direct – Flawed	100	Induced Cracking	005	4 days	Direct Through Port
COGA10	Oil –Direct – Flawed	100	Induced Cracking	006	5 days	Direct Through Port
COGA11	Oil –Direct – Flawed - Dropped	100	Induced Cracking + 1 m drop	007	5 days	Direct Through Port
COGA12	Oil –Direct – Flawed - Clogged	50	Induced Cracking + Simulated Clogged Filter	X1	4 days	Direct Through Port

[a] The contaminant oil was the same for every test: Aliphatic hydrocarbon petroleum-based hydraulic oil manufactured by Coilhose Pneumatics, Inc. (CAS# 64742-58-1 and 64742-62-7).

5.1 Test 1: Raw Candle Material Tests

This test was a simple full scale test of a candle brick that was removed from its container and subjected to impact energies in excess of the 10 ft-lb (13.4 J) used in the small scale impact tests. The purpose of the test was to determine if the porous material of the candle with oil will ignite or react when subjected to impact. This was deemed important as an aid to determining how to handle suspect candles should oil contamination be present and if the candles posed a significant drop hazard.

The solid candle brick was removed from the canister and placed directly on a steel plate. This is considered a worse case condition since the brick is normally protected from sudden sharp impacts by the metal canister and Kaowool insulation.

The test used a simple method of dropping a weight of known mass from a set height. The test was conducted remotely and observed via closed circuit television and high-speed cameras. The drop weight was activated remotely and allowed to drop onto a vertically positioned candle with oil saturating the top 10 percent of the brick. The mass of the weight was 500 lb (226.8 kg) dropped from a height of 2 ft

(0.61 m). This induced an impact level of 1000 ft-lb (1340 J), or 100 times the energy level of the small scale drop weight test's lowest recorded activation energy.

5.1.1   Test Summary

Test Designator: COGA1

Test Objectives:
- To determine the procedures needed to work safely with contaminated SCOGs
- To assess degree of shock sensitivity of contaminated SCOGs (small test samples of contaminated chlorate material were shock sensitive at the lowest level impact on the standard impact test)

Test Configuration:
- Chemical briquette was removed from metal canister.
- Upper 10 percent of the briquette was contaminated with oil.
- Contamination was at or near stoichiometric mixture.
- 500 lb weight located ~ 2 ft above chemical briquette.
- Chemical briquette was initially unfractured.

Event Sequence:
- Chemical briquette was positioned in free-standing configuration.
- Liquid oil was added to the top of the candle brick material via a remote fill system and allowed to disperse into the material for 24 h.
- A square-bottomed 500 lb weight was dropped directly onto the top surface of the candle brick.
- No exothermic reaction occurred.
- Brick buckled near mid-section forming two separate masses.

Discussion and Results:
- Contaminated material in this configuration did not produce a reaction from direct impact loading at the level used.
- Lack of confinement and inability to generate sufficient heat appeared to prevent reaction from starting in this configuration.
- The void space in the chemical briquette is such that when the voids were filled with liquid oil, the chlorate/oil mixture was nearly stoichiometric.
- The small scale samples used powered brick material, uniformly distributed oil, and rigid confinement. The porous brick material and more heterogeneous condition appear to be the leading factors in preventing sufficient heat build-up to cause an ignition.

5.1.2   Posttest Observations/Conclusions

- The lack of confinement and the degree of homogeneity affected the shock or impact sensitivity of sodium chlorate and oil mixtures in this configuration.
- The brick form of the material, when saturated to near stoichiometry, was not shock sensitive at the level of impact used (~ 1000 ft-lb, 1340 J) despite being removed from the canister and placed on a steel impact surface.

5.2   Test 2: SCOG26 with Oil Added via Filter Holes, No Known Flaws

The next test in the series was the first full scale test of an oil-contaminated candle. The purpose for this test was to take a known quantity of oil and allow it to percolate through the filtration exhaust ports, through the Hopcalite filter material, and drip into the canister. This allowed the examination of one possible entry path resulting from a broken or removed seal, letting oil collect on the can lid and enter the container over a period of time.

The path of oil travel required the filter medium to saturate with oil, thus a portion of the total oil was trapped in the filter. This test configuration also partially blocked or impeded the primary escape route for gases generated from the reaction.

The test used 400 mL (13.5 oz) of oil added to the top of the SCOG26 and allowed to flow through the filter over a 3-h time period.

This test was conducted in winter months. The test article had loosely wrapped 'heater tape' on the upper half of the canister to maintain temperatures above 40 °F (4.4 °C) during oil addition.

5.2.1 Test Summary

Test Designator: COGA2

Test Objectives:
- To safely conduct a test of a SCOG26 contaminated with large amounts of oil
- To verify methods of remote actuation, high-speed photography, and thermocouple data collection
- To make an initial evaluation of a highly contaminated SCOG26

Test Configuration:
- Full scale SCOG26
- 400 mL of oil was poured onto the lid of the SCOG, where it seeped through the vent ports into the filter material, and then onto the chemical briquette.
- Ignition used the standard .410 igniter cartridge, remotely actuated using a solenoid driven striker.
- SCOG26 was unconfined and free-standing.
- Chemical briquette was initially unfractured.

Event Sequence:
- The .410 cartridge was initiated (remotely).
- Hissing sound occurred.
- Reaction occurred inside the canister at a significantly increased rate of gas production.
- Oil from the filter was forced onto the outside of the canister and began to burn on the external surface of the canister (Figure 7).
- "Blow torch" behavior resulted in 50 percent melting of the solenoid housing (Figure 9).
- Canister did not burst, but the upper surface of the canister burned through.
- Large amounts of white vapor were formed.

Figure 7
Flame Ejecting from Top Vent Ports

Figure 8
Blow Torch Behavior and Solenoid Melting

Discussion and Results:

- 400 mL of oil was applied to the candle, but the fill procedure "overflowed" and 200 to 300 mL entered the candle and the rest spilled over the "lip" of the candle.
- Of the oil that entered the candle, much of it remained in the filter section, and an unspecified amount contaminated the chemical briquette, estimated at 100 to 200 mL.
- Test resembled an oxygen-enhanced fuel burn (like a torch) (Figure 8).
- The upper surface of the canister burned through, and the solenoid housing was ~ 50 percent melted.

5.2.2   Posttest Observations/Conclusions

- There was a significant increase in reaction rate and gas/heat production compared to a nominal candle.
- Pressure time rise was insufficient to cause canister rupture.
- Flames burned through the upper surface of the canister and melted ~ 50 percent of the striker body assembly.
- Candle behaved in a "blow torch" or rocket-motor-like behavior.
- Material acted in a manner similar to solid rocket propellant.

5.3   Test 3: SCOG26 with Oil Added via Filter Holes, No Known Flaws

The next test in the series attempted to increase the reaction rate by adding more oil than the first test and allowing additional time to allow oil in the filter to drip into the container. The test used 600 mL (20.3 oz) of oil added incrementally to the top of the SCOG26 and allowed to flow through the filter over a 4-day time period. This test was conducted in winter months. Therefore, a loosely wrapped 'heater tape' on the upper half of the canister was used to maintain temperatures above 40 °F (4.4 °C) during oil addition.

5.3.1   Test Summary

Test Designator: COGA3

Test Objective:
- To retest the COGA2 configuration with additional oil, and with more time for the oil to penetrate into the chemical briquette (COGA2 allowed the oil to penetrate for 3 h; COGA3 allowed the oil to penetrate 4 days)

Test Configuration:
- Full scale SCOG26
- 600 mL of oil was poured onto the lid of the SCOG, where it seeped through the vent ports into the filter material, and then onto the chemical briquette (Figure 9).
- Ignition used the standard .410 igniter cartridge, remotely actuated using a solenoid driven striker.
- SCOG26 was unconfined and free-standing.
- Chemical briquette was initially unfractured.
- Top half of SCOG26 was wrapped in heating tape to maintain test article temperature above 40 °F (4.4 °C) during 4-day soak time.

Figure 9
SCOG26 with Remote Solenoid Activator and Remote Oil Fill System

Event Sequence:

- The .410 cartridge was initiated (remotely).
- Hissing sound occurred.
- Pressure relief valves activated (Time Sequence 1).
- Flames came out of vent ports and relief valves (Time Sequence 2, 3) (Figure 10).
- Canister bulged (Time Sequence 2, 3). (Note: Bulging was partially confined along the top half of the canister by the heat tape used to maintain above-freezing conditions in cold weather for the 4-day oil addition cycle.)
- Canister breaches occurred at the base of the canister (Time Sequence 4).
- Canister launched upward "like a rocket," reaching ~ 370 ft/s (250 mph) in about 10 ms, average acceleration about 1250 g (Time Sequence 4,5,6,7).
- The "launching" canister impacted the 500 lb weight (with starting solenoid still attached) (Time Sequence 7).
- Enclosure began to fill almost completely with vapor 10 to 16 ms after breach (Time Sequence 7, 8).
- 14 ms after the breach, a secondary reaction zone at the location of the original base of the candle formed (Sequence 8).
- From 14 to 24 ms after the breach, a vapor cloud explosion (VCE) expanded at a rate of 1500 to 2000 ft/s (Time Sequence 9, 10).
- From 25 ms after breach onward, the camera sensors were saturated from VCE light emission.
- Entire area was filled with white smoke
- The chemical briquette and canister bottom remained stationary; only the canister, solenoid assembly, and filter assembly "rocketed" upward.
- Some of the chlorate material continued to burn for several minutes (secondary fires of oil-contaminated pieces).
- Some of the chlorate material remained unreacted, or self-extinguished.

Figure 10
Flame Behavior from Primary Vent Ports, Test 3

High Speed Video Imagery, Test 3 (Figures 11 and 12):

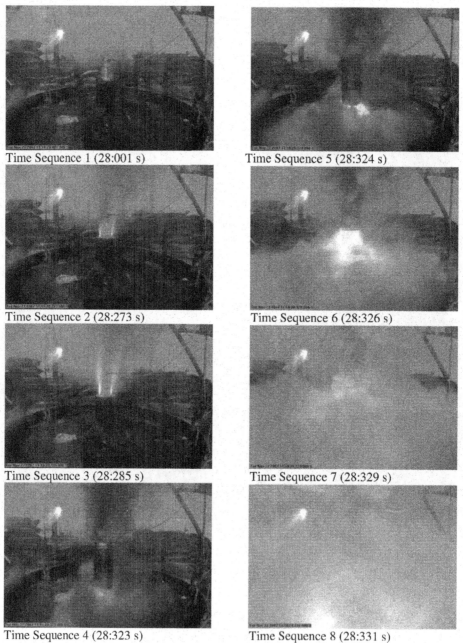

Time Sequence 1 (28:001 s)   Time Sequence 5 (28:324 s)

Time Sequence 2 (28:273 s)   Time Sequence 6 (28:326 s)

Time Sequence 3 (28:285 s)   Time Sequence 7 (28:329 s)

Time Sequence 4 (28:323 s)   Time Sequence 8 (28:331 s)

Figure 11
High Speed Video Frame Sequence Frames 1 through 8 (Test 3)

Time Sequence 9 (28:333 s)   Time Sequence 10 (28:335 s)

Figure 12
High Speed Video Frame Sequence Frames 9 and 10 (Test 3)

Long Range Camera Views (Test 3) (Figure 13):

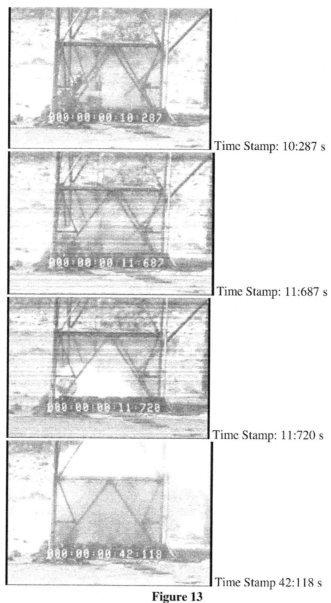

Time Stamp: 10:287 s

Time Stamp: 11:687 s

Time Stamp: 11:720 s

Time Stamp 42:118 s

Figure 13
Test 3: Selected Long Range Camera Views

Discussion and Results:
- It is unknown whether the test resulted in fast deflagration or detonation of VCE seen at 14 to 25 ms after initial breach.
- The entire sequence of events from canister breach to vapor cloud explosion and subsequent camera sensor overload occurred in about 25 ms.
- Canister broke into three primary fragments: one small fragment ripped off the base; the rest of the base remained intact; and the lid, filter plate and walls of the canister remained integrated despite partial failure of some seams and marked deformation (Figure 14).
- The solenoid assembly remained attached to the filter assembly and was pushed into the canister body by the force of impact into the weight.
- The canister impact on the overhanging weight had no effect on the test or secondary events.

Figure 14
Test 3: Overhead View of Ground Zero Debris

5.3.2 Hypothesis on Reaction

Photographic evidence of a secondary reaction occurring outside the canister and generating a light emitting region (fireball) was observed. The behavior is suspected to be a VCE or flash fire. The probability is high that remaining fuel and available oxidizer generated a thermobaric explosion from a region of rapidly vaporizing or pre-vaporized material at ground level, occurring ~16 ms after the canister breached. It is unknown if vapor formation was a direct result of BLEVE behavior external to the canister or if the vapors were already gaseous during the initial event expansion and material release phase.

Note: The entire sequence, from can separation, flight time, impact, filling of enclosure with vapor, and apparent VCE reaction required to fill the field of view, is estimated to be ~ 24 to 26 ms (12 to 13 frames at 2 ms per frame). For comparison, this is approximately one-quarter of the time, or four times faster, than a "blink of the human eye" (100 ms).

These events appear to be consistent with theoretical behavior for the types of materials and mechanisms described earlier. The speed of the event would appear instantaneous to a human observer, although several separate events occurred within the ~ 25-ms time frame.

5.3.3 Longer Duration Events

- Oil soaked sections of the candle, sufficiently heated and aflame, continued to burn for nearly 2 min prior to extinguishing. Posttest examination indicated these objects resulted in solidified puddles of salt material.
- Non-oil-doped candle material self-extinguished or failed to ignite outside the confines of the canister.
- No major fragmentation of the canister occurred.
- One small fragment ripped from the canister bottom (~0.5 by 1.5 in. (1 by 4 cm)).
- Remaining fragments showed only ductile bending or tearing; no brittle fracture was evident.
- Approximately two-thirds of the brick material was consumed during the initial reaction and the subsequent ~ 2 min of burning after the canister launched.
- Approximately one-third of the candle material remained, with the majority of the material being from the lower section of the brick. The remaining material was comprised primarily of non-oil-doped material (~ 75 percent) with the remaining (~25 percent) recovered material having evidence of at least some oil absorption.

5.3.4 Posttest Observations/Conclusions

- For the pristine candle with 600 mL oil, the reaction rate increased compared to the first test, but not at a rate sufficient to cause canister fragmentation from the internal pressurization. The sudden rocketing of the canister away from the reactants disallowed the examination of possible BLEVE fragmentation effects.
- Weak point/failure point appeared to be the lower weld area along the bottom rim of the canister.
- Photographic/film provided evidence of a secondary reaction occurring outside the canister, beginning 16 ms after the canister breach and generating a light emitting region (fireball). This is surmised to be a reaction of remaining fuel and available oxidizer in a thermobaric explosion from a region of rapidly vaporizing and/or vaporized material at ground level after ejection from the canister.
- Burning of assumed oil-contaminated brick material sections continued for ~ 2 min. Based on approximate size and shape of chunks and residual salt puddles, these regions experienced unconfined linear combustion rates of 1 to 2 in./min. This is roughly an order of magnitude increase in burn rate over nominal candle brick material burns while in normal operation.

33

- The bulk of the material acted in a manner similar to solid rocket propellant, both under confinement and unconfined.

5.4   Test 4: SCOG26 with 100 mL Oil Added via Center Port, Known Flaws

The next test in the series altered the method of oil introduction and added known flaws to the brick structure in an attempt to increase the surface area for reaction.

The scenario under investigation examined the possibility that the hydrocarbon may have entered through the primary ignition port in the SCOG26. When the SCOG26 protective lid is removed, a port to insert the igniter cartridge is exposed. This is a tube that extends through the filter material and allows direct access to the candle brick material and iron-enriched dome region.

The test method was altered to allow direct addition of oil to the top of the brick material. The wait time for diffusion/absorption was extended to 5 days prior to ignition.

The candle material was fractured by inserting a metal probe through the ignition port to induce cracks in the brick material. The SCOG26 was then X-rayed to determine the extent of cracking.
The amount of oil added to the SCOG26 was 100 mL (3.4 oz).

Test Designator: COGA4

Test Objectives:
- To test the effect of a fractured chemical briquette
- To conduct the first test where contamination is poured directly into the chemical briquette, so a more accurate measure of briquette contamination can be made

Test Configuration:
- Full scale SCOG26
- 100 mL of oil was poured directly into the chemical briquette through the ignition port
- Ignition used the standard .410 igniter cartridge, remotely actuated using a solenoid driven striker
- SCOG26 was unconfined and free-standing
- Chemical briquette was initially fractured (Figure 15)

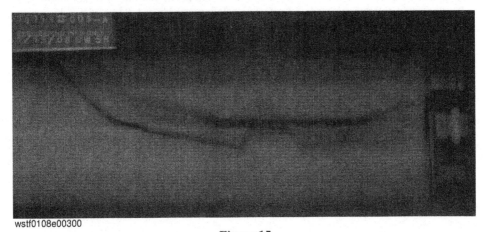

wstf0108e00300

Figure 15
Radiograph of COGA4 Test Article Primary Crack Zone (SN/003)

Event Sequence:
- The .410 cartridge was initiated (remotely, t = 0.0 s).
- Hissing sound occurred (Time Sequence 1).
- Canister began to bulge and pressure relief devices activated (t = 2.2 s).
- Flames began coming out the vent ports and relief valves (t = 2.52 s) (Time Sequence 2, 3) (Figure 16).
- Canister continued to bulge and flame jets continued to grow vertically from top ports (Time Sequence 4, 5).
- Canister bulging bowed the bottom of the candle, causing candle to rock slightly and then tip over (t = 3.00-3.85 s). Small laminar flames were seen on the outer surface of the canister body from apparent combustion of trace surface contaminants (Time sequence 6).
- The canister was momentarily stationary (t = 3.83 s) on its side before accelerating along the ground of the test cell to the edge of the lower containment ring (t = 3.85 – 4.16 s) with an average speed of 8 ft/s or less (Time Sequence 7) (Figure 17).
- The port jet flame region appeared to become nearly stationary at t = 4.16 s, indicating the canister had come to a halt at the edge of the containment ring (Time Sequence 8) (Figure 17).
- A bright flash of expanding light occurred and overwhelmed the camera sensors (t = 4.18 to 4.21 s), indicating a rapidly expanding reaction zone had formed and overwhelmed the camera sensors (Time Sequence 9).
- The top section breach and reaction at t = 4.18 s apparently accelerated the solenoid and canister in opposite directions, based on posttest examination.
- Light levels gradually subsided (t = 4.58 to 4.62 s).
- Another brief hemispherical expanding region of light began to form (t = 4.62 to 4.63) prior to fading.
- The bright reaction region within the cloud pulsated with moderate light output (t = 4.63 to 4.82 s), and a piece of insulation was floating (in left frame) undergoing combustion (Time Sequence 10).
- Another bright expanding region formed and again overwhelmed the camera sensors (t = 4.83 to 4.89 s) (Time Sequence 10-12) (Figure 17).
- Light levels once again subsided, allowing camera sensor recovery, and the remaining material smoked/burned for the duration of event (Time Sequence 13, 14) (Figure 18).
- Some chlorate material on the test cell floor continued to burn for several minutes. Some unreacted chlorate material on the test cell floor never ignited. Some of the chlorate material that remained inside the canister continued to react for more than 20 min.

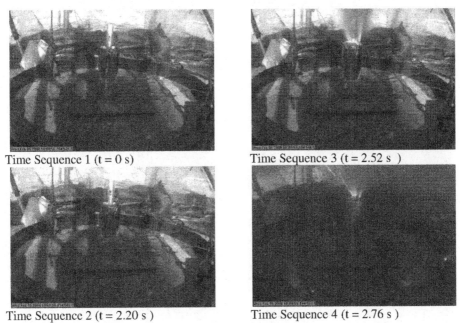

Time Sequence 1 (t = 0 s) Time Sequence 3 (t = 2.52 s)

Time Sequence 2 (t = 2.20 s) Time Sequence 4 (t = 2.76 s)

Figure 16
Initial Reaction through Primary Pressure Relief Ports and Vent Holes

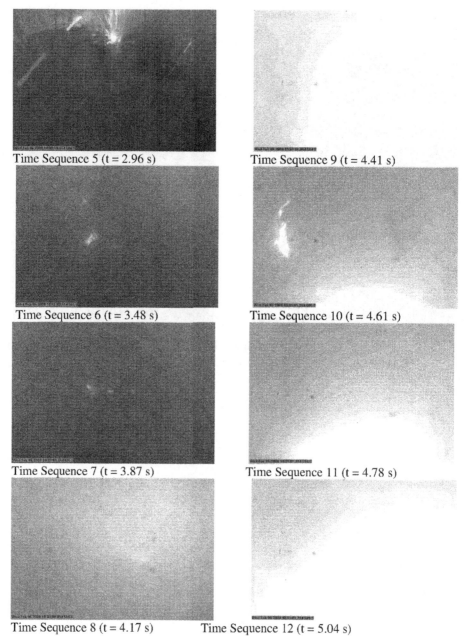

Time Sequence 5 (t = 2.96 s) Time Sequence 9 (t = 4.41 s)

Time Sequence 6 (t = 3.48 s) Time Sequence 10 (t = 4.61 s)

Time Sequence 7 (t = 3.87 s) Time Sequence 11 (t = 4.78 s)

Time Sequence 8 (t = 4.17 s) Time Sequence 12 (t = 5.04 s)

Figure 17
Canister "Tip-over," Movement across Enclosure, and VCE Events

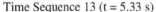

Time Sequence 13 (t = 5.33 s)   Time Sequence 14 (t = 6.91 s)

Figure 18
Flame Reduction and Residual Gas Cloud

Discussion and Results:

- Although the amount of oil used was less than COGA3, the reaction appeared faster, attributable to the fractured condition of the brick material.
- The fractured candle burst near the top (where the fractures were and where the reaction started) instead of the bottom of the candle.
- The reaction was sufficient to petal the filter plates outward and accelerate the solenoid assembly to sufficient velocity to dent the inner steel retaining ring and ricochet into the camera tripod housing and cause deformation of the metal housing with significant force.
- Posttest examination of the canister showed a significant concavity deformed the canister inward from an impact with a linear surface and a rounded end, based on the indentation shape (similar to a large "eyebolt" pattern). The degree of indentation (~ 1 in.) showed indication of significant force.
- The lack of any restraint on the candle allowed the bulging of the canister bottom to create an unstable shape and cause a tip-over.
- Damage and denting to the lower containment ring and housing on a camera tripod indicate the solenoid obtained significant velocity, believed to be during the primary energetic release event (Time Sequence 8, t = 4.17 s).
- Indentations on the canister bottom showed an impact occurred at a similar significant velocity, creating a concavity that suggests a significant primary energetic release event drove the canister into an object.
- Two additional energetic events occurred after the primary burst event.
- Canister fragment failure was ductile in nature. Most (> 90 percent) of the lid and all of the filter plate material were ejected, with the remainder of the lid still attached to the upper rim showing petal formation and ductile tears (Figure 19).
- Canister showed no signs of side wall breach.
- Coloration of the canister steel exterior indicated that the external temperature reached 900 to 1000 °F (480 to 540 °C) during the event.

Figure 19
Top Down View of Test 4 Aftermath

5.5 Test 5: SCOG26 with 100 mL Oil Added via Center Port, Known Flaws

The next test in the series was a repeat of the initial conditions from Test 4 except for the addition of a holder assembly. The SCOG26 produces heat during operation and normally placed in a holder to prevent personnel from coming into physical contact with the heated surfaces. The SCOG26 involved in the accident was in a holder partially constraining the device. A holder was used in this test to simulate the same conditions found during the initial accident.

The amount of oil added to the SCOG26 was 100 mL (3.4 oz). The oil soak time was 5 days.

5.5.1 Test Summary

Test Designator: COGA5

Test Objective:
- To test the effect of additional confinement caused by SCOG26 holder

Test Configuration:
- Full scale SCOG26
- 100 mL of oil was poured directly into the chemical briquette through the ignition port
- Ignition used the standard .410 igniter cartridge, remotely actuated using a solenoid driven striker
- SCOG26 was constrained by a holder similar to the SCOG26 holder involved in the accident
- Chemical briquette was initially fractured (similar amount of fracture as in COGA4) (Figure 20)

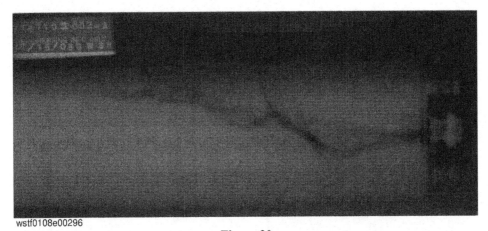

wstf0108e00296

Figure 20
Radiograph of COGA5 Test Article Primary Crack Zone (SN/002)

Event Sequence:
- The .410 cartridge was initiated (remotely) (t = 0.0 s)
- Hissing sound occurred
- White vapor began to flow out of primary vent ports (Time Sequence 1) (Figure 21)
- Pressure relief devices activated at ~0.6-0.70 s after initiation
- Canister bulging was noted into the openings of the holder just prior to burst
- Burst occurred 0.72 s after initiation (about 3 times faster than previous test COGA4 value of 2.2 s)
- Formation of fireball was seen immediately following initial burst (Time Sequence 2) (Figure 21)
- Lexan containment screens were blown off the test tower (Time Sequence 3-8) (Figures 21 and 22)
- Fragments were impacted into the Lexan containment screens
- Fragments were blown up to 120 ft from the test tower
- Some chlorate material on the test cell floor continued to burn for several minutes and some unreacted chlorate material on the test cell floor never ignited

40

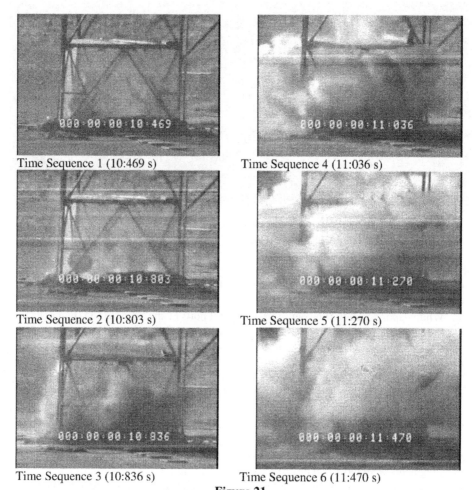

Time Sequence 1 (10:469 s)   Time Sequence 4 (11:036 s)

Time Sequence 2 (10:803 s)   Time Sequence 5 (11:270 s)

Time Sequence 3 (10:836 s)   Time Sequence 6 (11:470 s)

Figure 21
Test 5: Selected Long Range Camera Views of Primary Events

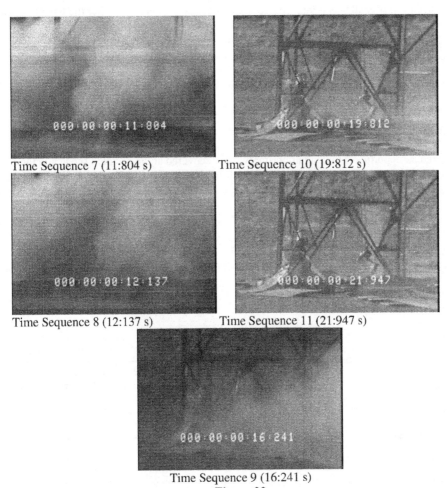

Time Sequence 7 (11:804 s)   Time Sequence 10 (19:812 s)

Time Sequence 8 (12:137 s)   Time Sequence 11 (21:947 s)

Time Sequence 9 (16:241 s)
Figure 22
Test 5: Selected Long Range Camera Views of Aftermath

Discussion and Results:
- This was a faster reaction overall than any previous test.
- High-speed deflagration behavior was observed.
- Equipment failure limited posttest analysis to 30 frames per second video.
- Reaction rate appeared to be increasing exponentially just prior to container burst.
- SCOG holder twisted and disassembled.
- Some of the 0.25-in.-thick Lexan sheeting used for containment screens shattered in a brittle fashion indicating a high strain rate event occurred.
- Fragments penetrating the Lexan indicated that energy levels of some fragments exceeded the ballistic rating of these sheets (Lexan of this thickness is rated to stop .22 caliber firearm rounds).
- Fragments were found at distances up to 120 ft from ground zero. Some pieces may have exceeded 150 ft and are still in the process of being located.
- 80 percent of all recovered fragments traveled less than 75 ft.
- Debris showed evidence of brittle failure on some fragments, ductile and shear failure on others.

- A reddish fireball was produced over the bottom of the enclosure after the burst, indicating that some of the fuel was still present and reacting.
- Data were inconclusive to determine if a secondary or tertiary blast type was involved (BLEVE or VCE); however, based on previous high-speed data and resulting pressure wave effects, one or both of these blast types is considered likely.
- Initial assessment is that COGA5 had many of the same attributes as the initial accident (BOI, 2008).

5.5.2 Direct Comparison to Accident, Histogram

COGA5 offered an opportunity to compare primary data recovered at the accident scene and the end results of Test 5. The energetic nature of the event and the widespread distribution of fragments in a desert environment precluded 100 percent recovery of canister debris.

- Accident scene investigators recovered 77 percent of the mass of the canister in the form of 57 fragments. COGA5 test recovered 73 percent of the mass of the canister in the form of 54 fragments.
- Mass distribution data are available from both the accident and the COGA5 test.

The size and distribution of recovered pieces allowed the creation of a histogram for direct comparison of the two events (Figure 23).

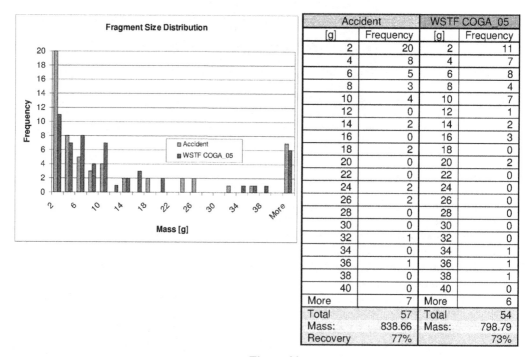

Accident		WSTF COGA_05	
[g]	Frequency	[g]	Frequency
2	20	2	11
4	8	4	7
6	5	6	8
8	3	8	4
10	4	10	7
12	0	12	1
14	2	14	2
16	0	16	3
18	2	18	0
20	0	20	2
22	0	22	0
24	2	24	0
26	2	26	0
28	0	28	0
30	0	30	0
32	1	32	0
34	0	34	1
36	1	36	1
38	0	38	1
40	0	40	0
More	7	More	6
Total	57	Total	54
Mass:	838.66	Mass:	798.79
Recovery	77%		73%

Figure 23
Histogram and Size Distribution Table

43

The accident and Test 5 canister failure produced similar size distributions. This indicates that the time of loading and energy levels between the two events are similar. Test 5 successfully recreated an event similar to the accident using 100 mL (3.4 oz) of fuel.

The following photos (Figures 24 through 27) are a direct comparison of the Test 5 fragments and fragments recovered from the scene of the original accident.

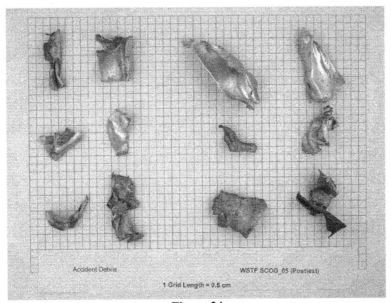

Figure 24
Test 5: Side-by-Side Comparison to Accident Fragments Set A

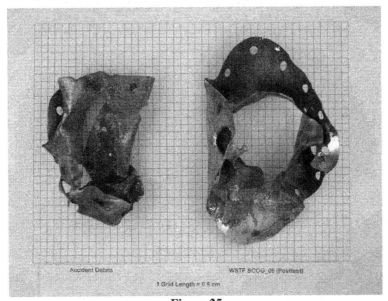

Figure 25
Test 5: Side-by-Side Comparison to Accident Fragments Set B

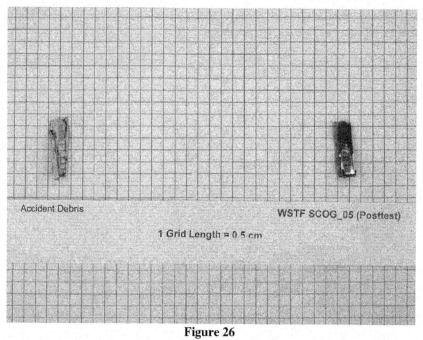

Figure 26
Test 5: Side-by-Side Comparison to Accident Fragments Set C

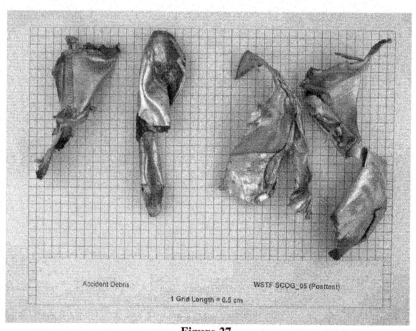

Figure 27
Test 5: Side-by-Side Comparison to Accident Fragments Set D

The overall pattern and manner of failure indicate similar stress-time loadings occurred in both events. The final conclusion is the Test 5 event was representative of the accident in both energy release magnitude and mechanisms involved.

5.5.3 Changes to Enclosure after Test 5

The near complete destruction of the Lexan enclosure required building a new enclosure and witness plate system. The option to use 0.5-in.-thick plywood hanging walls was chosen, and the result is shown in Figure 28.

wstf0308e02341

Figure 28
Plywood Enclosure and Witness Plate at Ground Zero Tests 6 through 12

5.6 Test 6: SCOG26 with 100 mL Oil Added via Center Port, No Known Flaws

The next test in the series was a repeat of the Test 5 holder configuration with a pristine SCOG26. Test 5 used an intentionally damaged SCOG26 to increase the internal surface area of the material. Test 6 used an undamaged SCOG26. The Lexan enclosure was replaced with a hanging plywood wall witness plate and fragment mitigation barrier design.

The amount of oil used was 100 mL (3.4 oz.). The oil soak time was 5 days.

Test Designator: COGA6

Test Objective:
- To test the effect of a SCOG holder containment on an unfractured candle

Test Configuration:
- Full scale SCOG26
- 100 mL of oil was poured directly into the chemical briquette through the ignition port.
- Ignition used the standard .410 igniter cartridge, remotely actuated using a solenoid driven striker.
- SCOG26 was constrained by a holder similar to the SCOG26 holder involved in the accident.

- Chemical briquette was initially unfractured.

Event Sequence:
- The .410 cartridge was initiated (remotely).
- Hissing sound occurred.
- Canister bulged.
- Pressure relief devices both activated near t = 2.08 s.
- Flames jets 2 to 4 in. in length formed at relief valves (t = 3.00 s), along with white vapor.
- Canister continued to bulge and spit flame from the relief valves.
- Relief valve fittings ejected from both sides of container nearly simultaneously, allowing a larger vent path to form (t = 3.98 s).
- Canister did not burst; however, flame sizes increased in spurts to lengths of 1 to 2 ft (t = 3.98 ~ 5.00 s) (Figures 29 and 30).
- Flames diminished to 1 to 2 in. again (t = 5.2+ s) as canister bulging decreased over same time span.
- SCOG continued to decompose nominally until remaining briquette was consumed.

Test Imagery:

Figure 29
Flame and Vapor at t = 4.182 s
(Note: Pressure relief device top piece in flight towards camera position at right center of flame plume)

47

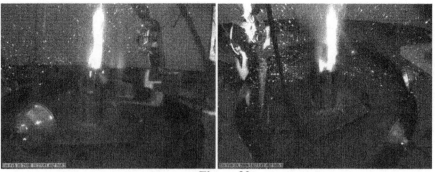
Figure 30
COGA6 Flames at t = 4.296 s (2 Views)

Discussion and Results:
- The SCOG holder caused an unfractured candle to remain in place.
- Bulging was evident prior to pressure relief device activation and pressure relief valve part ejection.
- Partial failure of pressure relief ports opened and increased vent path size.
- Evidence of high surface temperatures from canister oxidation during firing was similar to COGA4.
- Deformation was similar to COGA5 just prior to burst; however, a slower pressure ramp rate was observed and the pressure relief devices/ports allowed the canister to maintain integrity (Figure 31).
- Gas production rate of COGA6 appeared to be ~ one-third the rate seen in COGA5, based on relief valve opening times of ~ 2.08 and 0.70 s respectively.
- Gas pressurization rate suggested a probable one-third less reaction surface area in the pristine candle versus the cracked COGA5 during the initial combustion prior to pressure relief valve activation.
- The reaction of COGA6 was energetic, and a burst event was deemed highly probable had the pressure relief devices not functioned.
- The end result was behavior more like a solid rocket motor for the primary energetic material phase combustion event prior to reverting to a more normal decomposition phase for the remainder of the test.

Figure 31
COGA6 Posttest View

49

5.7   Test 7: SCOG26 with 25 mL Oil Added via Center Port, Known Flaws

The energetic reaction from Test 5 used 100 mL of oil, a SCOG26 with known flaws, and partial confinement. Test 7 was designed to repeat Test 5 except using only 25 mL of oil instead of 100 mL. This test was an attempt to determine a lower bound for added fuel that could cause a catastrophic failure and ascertain the degree of contamination required to alter the SCOG26 from a relatively benign oxygen generator to a potentially lethal hazard.

The amount of oil used was 25 mL (0.85 oz). The soak time was 5 days.

Test Designator: COGA7

Test Objective:
- To test the effect of a SCOG holder containment on an fractured candle with 25 mL of oil

Test Configuration:
- Full scale SCOG26
- 25 mL of oil was poured directly into the chemical briquette through the ignition port.
- Ignition used the standard .410 igniter cartridge, remotely actuated using a solenoid driven striker.
- SCOG26 was constrained by a holder similar to the SCOG26 holder involved in the accident.
- Chemical briquette was initially fractured (Figure 32).

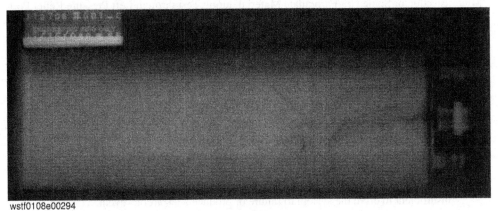

wstf0108e00294

Figure 32
Radiograph of COGA7 Test Article Primary Crack Zone (SN/001)

Event Sequence:
- The .410 cartridge was initiated (remotely).
- Hissing sound occurred.
- Canister bulged.
- One of two pressure relief devices activated, and some particulate was seen exiting the port (Figure 33).
- No major breach or vapor was formed.
- The SCOG26 continued to produce oxygen in the same manner and time frame as an uncontaminated SCOG26.

Figure 33
Minor Ejection of Some Hot Particulate Material during Test through Left Pressure Relief Port

Discussion and Results:
- The SCOG26 exhibited some of the characteristics of fuel contamination behavior, but to a lesser degree than previous tests.
- Gas production increased beyond nominal operation and some bulging of the canister was evident.
- Thermal output in the region of oil addition indicated a localized heating of the external surface sufficient to allow oxidization of the surface, as indicated by blue to straw-colored discoloration near the top of the canister (Figure 34).
- Some extrusion of top filter material through primary vent ports was observed, but no escaping Hopcalite material was evident (Figure 35).
- 25 mL of oil appeared to enhance the off-nominal behavior; however, the amount was insufficient to drive the system to failure or produce a hazardous event.

wstf0308e01672

Figure 34
Posttest SCOG26 in Holder with Thermal Discoloration (Test 7)

wstf0308e01676

Figure 35
Close-up View of Top of SCOG26 (Test 7) with Extruded Material at Vents

5.8   Test 8: SCOG26 with 100 mL Oil Added via Center Port, Known Flaws

Test 8 was conducted to attempt to recreate the results of Test 5. Test 5 showed, under the proper conditions of additional fuel, partial confinement, and increased surface area within the canister, that it was possible to overdrive the system to cause a rapid event or series of events that result in catastrophic failure of not only the SCOG26 but also the holder and nearby structures.

The amount of oil used was 100 mL (3.5 oz.). The soak time was 5 days.

Test Designator: COGA8

Test Objectives:
- To test the effect of a SCOG holder containment on an fractured candle with 100 mL of oil
- To recreate the conditions and effects of Test 5

Test Configuration:
- Full scale SCOG26
- 100 mL of oil was poured directly into the chemical briquette through the ignition port.
- Ignition used the standard .410 igniter cartridge, remotely actuated using a solenoid driven striker.
- SCOG26 was constrained by a holder similar to the SCOG26 holder involved in the accident.
- Chemical briquette was initially fractured (Figure 36).

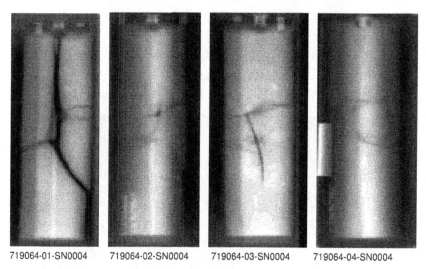

719064-01-SN0004   719064-02-SN0004   719064-03-SN0004   719064-04-SN0004

Figure 36
Radiographs of COGA8 Test Article Primary Crack Zone (SN/004)

Event Sequence:
- The .410 cartridge was initiated (remotely) at t = 0.018 s.
- Hissing sound occurred.
- Canister bulged visibly at t = 2.59 s.
- Pressure Relief device activated at t = 2.69 s.
- Hot gases and flames were observed exiting the top of the canister from the relief ports and filter holes (Figure 37).
- The solenoid striker assembly was ejected at t = 2.89 s.
- A pulsating flame and vapor ejection continued until 3.079 s.
- A sudden ejection of material and rapid expansion of a vapor and dust cloud were evident at 3.079 s with visible regions of combustion. Posttest evidence suggests the lower filter plate was ejected from within the container at this time and forced through the opening at the top of the canister (Figure 38).
- A moderate pressure pulse was observed reacting with the camera housing at t = 3.111 s, as evidenced by image movement within the field of view (camera enclosure oscillation).
- Flames continued to erupt from the SCOG26, and several pulsed fireball expansions (VCE) several feet in diameter were observed after the main ejection event at t = 3.079 s (Figure 39).
- The flames and vapor subsided after ~4 s, with the remaining material retaining enough heat to continue the nominal decomposition of sodium chlorate in the canister.
- The enclosure was filled with a white-gray cloud of vapor prior to dissipating from ventilation.

Figure 37
Pyrotechnic Behavior through Vent Ports and Canister Bulging into Holder (Test 8)

Figure 38
Primary Material Ejection Event (t = 3.079 s) with Moderate Pressure Pulse

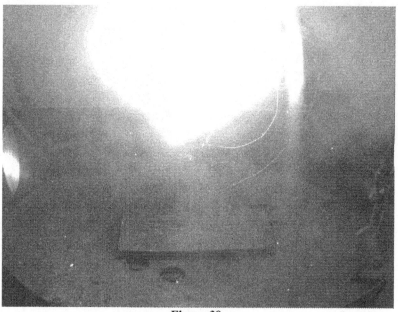

Figure 39
Fireball Formation (VCE) (t = 3.446 s)

Discussion and Results:
- The SCOG26 exhibited violent pyrotechnic-like behavior.
- Gas production increased beyond nominal operation, and some bulging of the canister was evident prior to pressure relief valve activation.
- In comparison to previous testing, the time to build pressure was delayed to over 2.5 s. This behavior is attributed to the location of the oil with respect to the ignition point and the relative surface area of the oil-enriched region being further from the primary ignition source.
- The inner filter plate was found to be severely deformed, and it was ejected violently from the SCOG26 along with the solenoid striker and some candle material.
- There is evidence of a secondary pressure wave behavior after the top of the candle began venting.
- The flames receded just prior to a burst of material, which is attributed to a rapid buildup of internal pressure near the center of the canister with a high degree of probability of being a BLEVE type event that forced the material and filter plate through the top of the canister (Figure 40).
- Several fireball events several feet in diameter occurred in the escaping vapor and particulate cloud.
- The sidewalls and bottom of canister remained intact.
- Posttest examination revealed only the top section of the canister had burned through, and the ductilely deformed filter plate was ejected from the hole created (Figure 41).

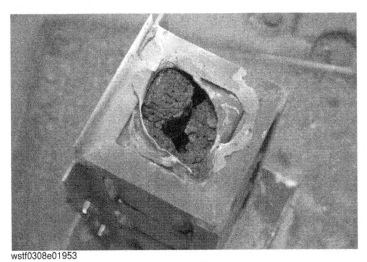

wstf0308e01953

Figure 40
Top of SCOG26 (Test 8)

wstf0308e01955

Figure 41
Ductilely Deformed Filter Plate

5.9   Test 9: SCOG26 with 100 mL Oil Added via Center Port, Known Flaws

Test 9 was conducted to attempt to recreate the results of Test 5. Test 8 showed that SCOG26 behavior is variable even when conditions are similar. Exact duplication of the conditions of Test 5 cannot be controlled precisely due to the variability in the method of inducing flaws into the brick material. It is impossible to predict how cracks will form within the material and the exact path the oil will take once inside the container. This leads to variations in the concentration and location of oil-enriched material and its relative location to the initial ignition source.

Test 9 attempted to examine variations in crack patterns to determine if a predictive method of behavior could be found based on apparent location and type of crack formation gathered from radiographic examination. The attempt was made to create cracks deep within the structure.

The amount of oil used was 100 mL (3.5 oz.). The soak time was 5 days.

Test Designator: COGA9

Test Objectives:
- To test the effect of a SCOG holder containment on an fractured candle with 100 mL of oil
- To recreate the conditions and effects of Test 5
- To examine effects of varying crack density and location

57

Test Configuration:
- Full scale SCOG26
- 100 mL of oil was poured directly into the chemical briquette through the ignition port.
- Ignition used the standard .410 igniter cartridge, remotely actuated using a solenoid driven striker.
- SCOG26 was constrained by a holder similar to the SCOG26 holder involved in the accident.
- Chemical briquette was initially fractured (Figure 42).

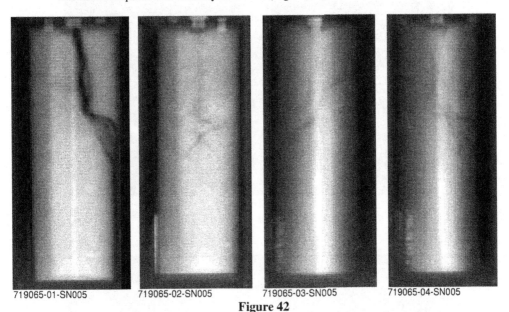

719065-01-SN005   719065-02-SN005   719065-03-SN005   719065-04-SN005

Figure 42
Radiographs of COGA9 Test Article Primary Crack Zone (SN/005)

Event Sequence:
- The .410 cartridge was initiated (remotely).
- Hissing sound occurred.
- Canister bulged.
- Pressure relief devices opened at t = 0.558 s.
- Ejection of vapor and particulate from vent ports began (t = 0.750 s).
- Flames and pyrotechnic-like behavior (t = 0.750 to 1.066 s) (Figure 43).
- Top of canister breached and ejection of material and vapor increased (t = 1.068 s) along with a fireball several feet in diameter (Figure 44).
- The camera enclosures were shaken by a moderate pressure pulse accompanying the breach and first fireball event.
- Several smaller fireball events occurred in escaping cloud, and vapor thickened in enclosure (t = 1.069 – 1.340 s), along with continued pyrotechnic-like behavior.
- Flames died down and candle burned for remainder of test (t = 1.34+ s).

Figure 43
Pyrotechnic Behavior, Test 9 (t = 1.000 s)

Figure 44
Primary Ejection Event, Test 9 (t = 1.068 s)

Discussion and Results:
- The SCOG26 exhibited violent pyrotechnic-like behavior.
- Gas production increased beyond nominal operation, and some bulging of the canister was evident prior to pressure relief valve activation.
- The event was similar to Test 8, with pyrotechnic behavior and ejection of material.
- The inner filter plate was found to be severely deformed and was ejected violently from the SCOG26 with some candle material.
- There was evidence of a secondary pressure wave behavior during the ejection event.
- Several fireball events, several feet in diameter, occurred in the escaping vapor and particulate cloud.
- The sidewalls and bottom of the canister remained intact.
- The solenoid striker remained attached to the peeled-back lid portion (Figure 45).
- Posttest examination revealed only the top section of the canister had burned through and the filter plate was ejected from the hole created.

wstf0308e02112

Figure 45
Posttest View of Top of SCOG26 (Test 9)

5.10   Test 10: SCOG26 with 100 mL Oil Added via Center Port, Known Flaws

Test 10 was another attempt to both recreate Test 5 behavior and examine the effects of crack density and location. The same configuration and fuel contamination level as Tests 5, 8, and 9 were employed to compare results.

The amount of oil used was 100 mL (3.5 oz). The soak time was 5 days

Test Designator: COGA10

Test Objectives:
- To test the effect of a SCOG holder containment on an fractured candle with 100 mL of oil

- To recreate the conditions and effects of Test 5
- To examine effects of varying crack density and location

Test Configuration:
- Full scale SCOG26
- 100 mL of oil was poured directly into the chemical briquette through the ignition port
- Ignition used the standard .410 igniter cartridge, remotely actuated using a solenoid driven striker
- SCOG26 was constrained by a holder similar to the SCOG26 holder involved in the accident
- Chemical briquette was initially fractured (Figure 46)

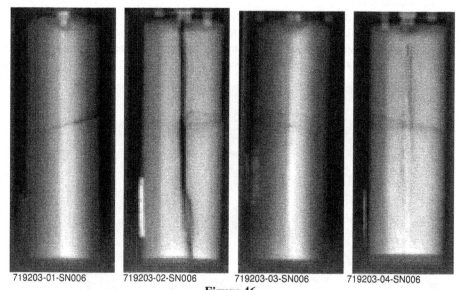

719203-01-SN006   719203-02-SN006   719203-03-SN006   719203-04-SN006

Figure 46
Radiographs of COGA10 Test Article Primary Crack Zone (SN/006)

Event Sequence:
- The .410 cartridge was initiated (remotely).
- Hissing sound occurred.
- Canister bulged.
- The pressure relieve devices activated at t = 0.645 s after initiation.
- Small flames and particulate continued to eject from pressure relief ports from t = 0.645 to 0.855 s.
- Vapors and particulate began to eject through the primary vent paths at t = 0.855 s.
- Pyrotechnic behavior increased and remained until t = 1.250 s before flames nearly disappear (Figure 47).
- Material was ejected in a burst of vapor and particulates at t = 1.263 s, accompanied by a pressure wave that shook the camera enclosures (Figure 48).
- Vapor density in enclosure increased.
- Flames died down at t = 1.590 s, and material continued to burn inside the canister to test completion.

Figure 47
Pyrotechnic Behavior Test 10 (t = 0.957 s)

Figure 48
Primary Ejection Event Test 9 (t = 1.263 s)

Discussion and Results:

- The SCOG26 exhibited violent pyrotechnic-like behavior.
- Gas production increased beyond nominal operation, and some bulging of the canister was evident prior to pressure relief valve activation.
- The event was similar to Test 8 and Test 9, with pyrotechnic behavior and ejection of material.
- The inner filter plate was found to be severely deformed and was ejected violently from the SCOG26 with some candle material.
- There is evidence of a secondary pressure wave behavior during the ejection event.
- Some minor fireball events were seen after the primary ejection event.
- The sidewalls and bottom of canister remained intact.
- The solenoid striker was ejected vertically.
- Posttest examination revealed only the top section of the canister had burned through (Figure 49), and the filter plate was ejected from the hole created (Figure 50).

wstf0308e02325

Figure 49
Top View of SCOG26 (Test 10)

wstf0308e02327

Figure 50
Ductilely Deformed Filter Plate (Test 10)

5.11   Test 11: SCOG26 with 100 mL Oil Added via Center Port, Known Flaws

Test 11 differed from the previous tests in one major variable. A holder identical to the holder in the original accident was obtained and used to mock-up the accident scenario as closely as possible. The previous energetic release of Test 5 was still used as the baseline for the amount of fuel contamination (100 mL, 3.4 oz) and suspected level of internal surface area (cracking). The goal of the test was to see if all the variables could be matched between Test 5 and the accident, to recreate the event as closely as possible.

One additional test was performed on COGA11 to determine the susceptibility of the brick material to further cracking by performing a single drop test. This test involved radiographing the candle after the initial crack induction, dropping COGA11 from 1 m (3.1 ft) vertically onto a concrete surface, and re-radiographing COGA11 to check for additional crack formation.

There was no discernable change between the two sets of radiographs.

The amount of oil used was 100 mL (3.4 oz). The soak time was 5 days.

Test Designator: COGA11

Test Objectives:
- To test the effect of a SCOG holder containment on an fractured candle with 100 mL of oil
- To recreate the conditions and effects of Test 5
- To examine effects of varying crack density and location
- To examine the effects of dropping a SCOG26 from a height of 1 meter on a hard surface

Test Configuration:
- Full scale SCOG26
- 100 mL of oil was poured directly into the chemical briquette through the ignition port.
- Ignition used the standard .410 igniter cartridge, remotely actuated using a solenoid driven striker.
- SCOG26 was free-standing and confined by a dual SCOG26 holder in the rightmost holder (Figures 51 and 52).
- Chemical briquette was initially fractured (Figure 53).

wstf0508e03658

Figure 51
Standard SCOG26 Holder Assembly
(Note: Front Panel Not Used In Tests 11 and 12)

wstf0408e02464

Figure 52
"Dummy" SCOG26 (Left) and COGA11 Test Article (Right)
in Standard Dual SCOG26 Holder (as Tested)

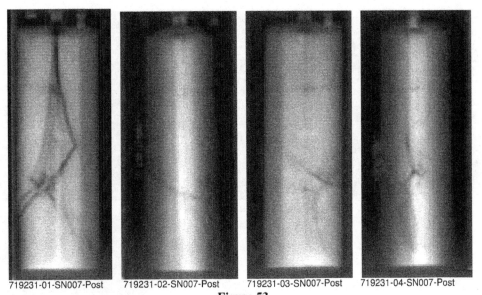

719231-01-SN007-Post   719231-02-SN007-Post   719231-03-SN007-Post   719231-04-SN007-Post

Figure 53

Radiographs of COGA11 Test Article Primary Crack Zone (SN/007, Post-drop Condition)

Event Sequence:
- The .410 cartridge was initiated (remotely).
- Hissing sound occurred.
- Canister bulged.
- The pressure relief devices activated at t = 1.152 s.
- Evidence of gas and particulate escaping from primary vent ports and through pressure relief devices at t = 1.152 to 1.196 s.
- The top seam on the canister began to open at t = 1.197 s.
- At t = 1.197 to 1.216 s a cloud was ejected at a rate of~ 1000 ft/s, consisting of vapor, particles, and signs of localized combustion, filling the camera view (less than 20 ms) (Figure 54).
- Camera was completely saturated from fireball at t = 1.217 s.
- Primary fireball faded at t = 1.248 s (0.050 s after initial seam split).
- At t = 1.253 s, the top of the SCOG26 was visible through dense white and gray smoke, and the top of the canister had been ripped back to expose the top portion of the brick, and flames were visible in the canister.
- At t = 1.260 s, candle material was seen emerging from the canister.
- At t = 1.285 s, a fireball began to form within the canister, and a large portion of the remaining brick material was ejected upward from the canister (Figure 55). This appeared to be a rapid gas expansion driving material from the canister, originating near the bottom of the SCOG26.
- The candle continued to smolder for the remainder of the test.

t = 1.198 s (Initial Burst)

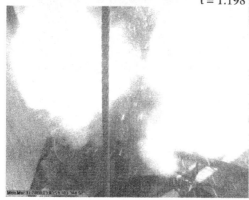 

t = 1.204 s (VCE Formation)

t = 1.212 s (VCE Fills View)

Figure 54
Primary Burst and VCE Formation

Figure 55
Second Fireball Formation and Brick Material Ejection (t = 1.363 s)

Discussion and Results:

- Gas production increased beyond nominal operation, and some bulging of the canister was evident prior to pressure relief valve activation.
- This first test using the standard SCOG26 holder showed most of the same general behavior as previous tests; however, the failure point was different and formed at the top front seam of the lid, allowing the top of the canister to peel back and remain attached to the canister (Figure 56).
- Several fireball events several feet in diameter occurred in the escaping vapor and particulate cloud.
- The sidewalls and bottom of canister remained intact.
- The majority of the candle brick was forced to eject from the canister, indicating a pressure buildup near the bottom of the canister.
- The pressure buildup is attributed to a BLEVE-like reaction near the bottom of the canister to drive the brick material out of the vertically standing SCOG26.
- The crack pattern in the COGA11 test article did have a path for fuel to flow towards the bottom of the canister, which is considered the likely reason for a reaction near the bottom of the canister.

wstf0408e02481   wstf0408e02480

Figure 56
Posttest 11 (2 views)

5.12 Test 12: SCOG26 with 50 mL Oil Added via Center Port, Known Flaws

Test 12 was the final test in the series. The lessons learned in previous testing indicated that:

- Increased cracking leads to increased surface area and increased gas production rate
- Restricted flow leads to increased pressurization rate
- Relatively small amounts of fuel can lead to undesired response in behavior

This last test in the series was used to aid in determining if a lower level of contamination than used in Test 5, coupled with a restricted vent path and a more granulated cracking of the brick near the top of the SCOG26, could lead to a catastrophic failure. To this end, the following steps were conducted to prepare the SCOG26:

- Increase cracking in the region near the top of the candle to form numerous high surface area pieces near the point of oil addition
- Decrease the amount of oil used from 100 to 50 mL (3.4 to 1.7 oz)
- Restrict the vent path by partial clogging of oxygen vent ports with a wood glue and water mixture
- Delay the pressure relief device response by adding an epoxy resin plug in the port relief path

These conditions simulate a case were the oil may have passed into the filter and partially clogged the vent paths over time. The increased cracking was provided to match some reports of SCOG26 candles removed from service and found to "rattle" when shaken, indicating partial granulation of the brick material.

The amount of oil used was 50 mL (1.7 oz). The soak time was 4 days.

Test Designator: COGA12

Test Objectives:
- To test the effect of a SCOG holder containment on an fractured candle with 50 mL of oil
- To examine effects of varying crack density and location
- To examine the effect of severe cracking near the top of the candle
- To examine the effect of partially restricted flow through filter ports and blocked pressure relief ports

Test Configuration:
- Full scale SCOG26
- 50 mL of oil was poured directly into the chemical briquette through the ignition port.
- Ignition used the standard .410 igniter cartridge, remotely actuated using a solenoid driven striker.
- SCOG26 was free-standing and confined by a dual SCOG26 holder in the rightmost holder.
- Chemical briquette was initially fractured (Figure 57).
- A spent SCOG26 was placed in the leftmost position in the dual SCOG26 holder to simulate the accident configuration.

Event Sequence:
- The .410 cartridge was initiated (remotely).
- Hissing sound occurred.
- Canister bulged significantly (t = 0.718 s).
- Some vapor particulate emerged from partially blocked vent holes (t = 0.724 to 0.736 s) (Figure 58).
- Burst began and formed a fireball ~ 2 ft across (t = 0.738 s) (Figure 59).
- Fireball had expanded to fill camera view (several feet across) in the next 2 ms (t = 0.740) (Figure 60).
- Debris and dark gray vapor filled camera view (t = 0.742 s).
- Large amounts of vapor were evident.
- Part of the SCOG26 holder side cover ejected through the door.

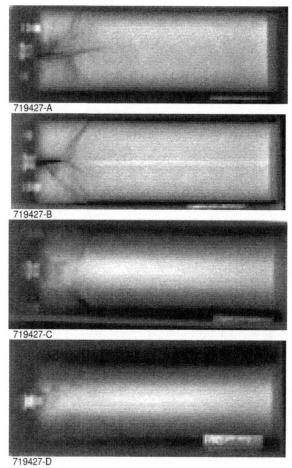

719427-A

719427-B

719427-C

719427-D

Figure 57
Radiographs of COGA12 Test Article Primary Crack Zone (SN/X1)

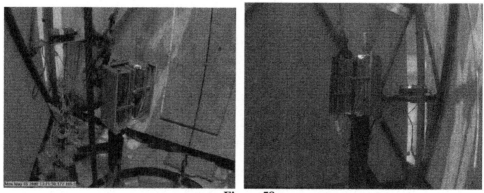

Figure 58
Vapor through Partially Blocked Vent Ports (t = 0.736 s)

Figure 59
Burst, Ejection of Material, and Ignition (t = 0.738 s)

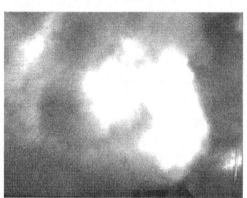

Figure 60
Primary Fireball (t = 0.740 s)

Discussion and Results:

- Gas production increased beyond nominal operation, and some bulging of the canister was evident prior to primary burst event.
- This second test, using the standard SCOG26 holder and partially blocked vent ports, resulted in significant damage that was similar in nature to Test 5 and the accident.
- Several square feet of the interior walls near the test article showed signs of severe thermal loads (plywood scorched and blackened) (Figure 61).
- The metal grating on the side of the SCOG holder closest to the test article was driven through the door and found 165 ft from ground zero, and the door was blown out.
- The holder was deformed in a manner similar to the holder from the original accident.
- The overall fragment size distributions were qualitatively examined vs. Test 5 and the accident. Overall, the sizes were larger, indicating a relative energy release at levels below Test 5 and the accident.
- Numerous fragments were driven through or imbedded in the plywood walls in a manner similar to photographic evidence of the accident.
- The "dummy" SCOG26 showed evidence of significant near field pressure damage from the test article generated pressure waves (Figure 62).

wstf0508e03667

wstf0508e03668

wstf0508e03669

Figure 61
Test 12 Deformation of SCOG26 Holder and Plywood Scorch Marks

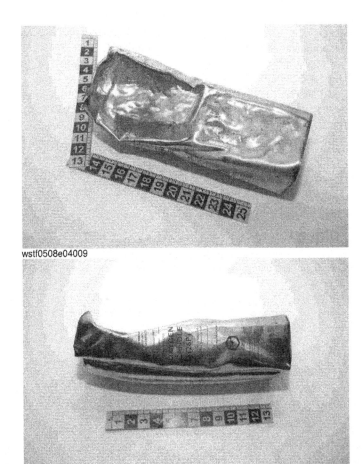

wstf0508e04009

wstf0508e04012

Figure 62
Recovered "Dummy" SCOG26 Test 12

5.13 Overall Test Review

The testing showed that a variety of conditions govern the ultimate reaction of the SCOG26 when exposed to hydrocarbon contamination. The primary factors found to be of importance are as follows:

- Amount of contamination
- Location of flaws within brick material
- Degree of surface area increase due to flaws
- Ability of pressure relief devices to control internal overpressure
- Degree of blocking of vent paths
- Ability of SCOG26 to form secondary explosive events including BLEVE and VCE under test conditions is probable based on test imagery

The next examination presented is with respect to timing of events during testing. The timing is divided into the following definitions:

74

- Pressure Valve Opening Time: This is the time after ignition for the pressure within a SCOG26 to reach the set point and activate the pressure relief devices.
- Primary Event: This is an event that breaches the container, producing a hazard level considered dangerous. This can be a burn-through event; an initial indication of ejection of material; or, in the case of Test 5 and Test 12, a single large explosive event or multiple events between data collection points (container breach only, container breach and BLEVE-like behavior).
- Secondary Event: This is either an event that ejects a large portion of the canister contents or components with an associated pressure pulse, or a gas cloud event with external fireball (BLEVE or VCE-like behavior observed).
- Tertiary Event: This is an energetic event that occurs external to the canister after a secondary ejection or fireball event has already occurred (VCE-like events).

The timing is plotted for each test in Figure 63.

Event Timing

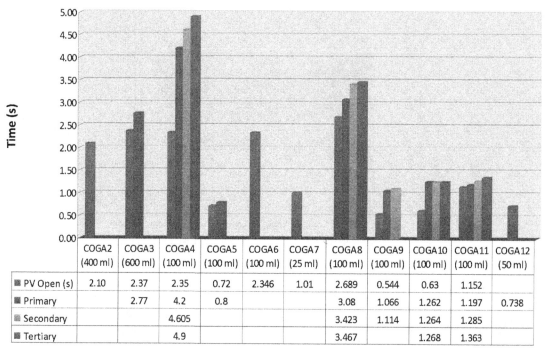

	COGA2 (400 ml)	COGA3 (600 ml)	COGA4 (100 ml)	COGA5 (100 ml)	COGA6 (100 ml)	COGA7 (25 ml)	COGA8 (100 ml)	COGA9 (100 ml)	COGA10 (100 ml)	COGA11 (100 ml)	COGA12 (50 ml)
PV Open (s)	2.10	2.37	2.35	0.72	2.346	1.01	2.689	0.544	0.63	1.152	
Primary		2.77	4.2	0.8			3.08	1.066	1.262	1.197	0.738
Secondary			4.605				3.423	1.114	1.264	1.285	
Tertiary			4.9				3.467		1.268	1.363	

Figure 63
Event Timing Chart

The general trends indicate that, once a SCOG26 is contaminated, the amount of time between ignition and potentially catastrophic events is only a few seconds. The initial breach of the container and subsequent events such as BLEVE or VCE occur in fractions of a second. The events that occurred in the accident are suspected to have followed a similar pattern and would not have allowed time for personnel to recognize and react prior to the lethal event.

The excessively contaminated SCOG26s (Test 2 and 3), and Tests 6 and 8 show a slower response than the remaining tests. Test 2, 3, and 6 are attributed to the pristine non-fractured candle effect on surface area, limiting the reaction rate. Test 8 is the only cracked candle that showed a delayed pressure relief device opening time. This is attributed to a large deep crack in this particular candle, allowing the initial oil to collect at a location away from the initial ignition point to a greater degree than the other tests.

The fastest reactions were found in Test 5 and 12, whose degree of cracking and close proximity of initial contamination to the initial ignition point are believed to be the primary cause of the most rapid pressurization rates.

6.0   Test Summary

The testing revealed the following and added to the base understanding of the behavior of solid fuel oxygen generators under off-nominal conditions.

- The addition of organic compounds of relatively low quantities (100 mL, 3.4 oz) could reproduce effects found in the original accident (as demonstrated in Test 5).
- Partial blocking or clogging of escape paths from excessive gas generation rates are more likely to produce lethal effects (Test 12) at lower levels of contamination (50 mL, 1.69 oz).
- Behavior with identical amounts of contamination and similar cracking can produce different results (Test 5 vs. Tests 8, 9, 10, and 11).
- Any addition of organic compounds into the mixture will produce undesirable effects.
- Gross contamination (400 and 600 mL, 13.5 and 20.3 oz) can produce catastrophic failure events with significant fireball formation (as demonstrated in Test 2 and 3).
- Fireball formation can occur with both large and small quantities of contamination.
- Test 12 showed that under certain conditions, a small quantity of contamination (50 mL, 1.7 oz) is adequate to produce a potentially lethal explosion and similar effects to Test 5 and the accident.
- 50 to 100 mL (1.7 to 3.4 oz) levels of contamination are deemed reasonable to have been present in the accident environment.

7.0   Conclusions and Recommendations

The analysis, simulation, and testing of SCOG26 oxygen candles has yielded many observations. Some conclusions are drawn directly from the data while others result from the application of the data to understand the damage reported from the HMS Tireless mishap. The latter has resulted in several recommendations. Throughout, attention has been paid to the vulnerability of similar systems designed for NASA spacecraft. Lastly, the authors offer their comments on chlorate-based systems for oxygen generation.

7.1   Objective, Data-based Conclusions

- SCOG26 devices have a long history of use. Some fires have been reported, none equal to the mishap aboard HMS Tireless.
- Organic material (Hydrocarbons) when mixed with Sodium Chlorate creates a fast-burning, potentially explosive material.
- Fragmentation (cracking) increases the rate of energy release in contaminated Chlorate material.

- Uncontaminated SCOG26, with cracked briquettes, (theoretically and in a limited number of trials[1]) burn nearly normally.
- A high probability exists for crack formation or partial granulation in a brittle brick material that is mishandled. Mishandling in turn increases the burn area of the canister contents. Depending on final particle/chunk size, the surface area can be increased many-fold with a similar increase in reaction rate possible. This is theorized to be the most likely combination to form a burn (thus pressurization) rate sufficient to cause a canister to burst with the observed overpressures.
- A relatively small amount of organic contamination in a SCOG26 will create a large amount of energetic material (the stoichiometric ratio being roughly 1:11), which can cause explosive gas generation and drive other explosive side processes.
- Lower quantities (less than stoichiometric) can still enhance burn rates by making large quantities of less energetic material that are still capable of generating explosions.
- Clogging (in part or whole) of the path of gas escape (either vents and/or relief devices) increases both the rate and amount of energy released for contaminated SCOG26.
- Physical restraint of the pressure canister, such as that provided by SCOG holders likely enhances the buildup of extreme pressure prior to rupture. This effect may drive side reactions farther, thus increasing the damage.
- The re-creation (Tests 5 and 12) of the effects described in the HMS Tireless Mishap support the hypothesis that if a SCOG26 is damaged and contaminated, the behavior of the SCOG26 can be capable of damage, injury, or death.
- The silicone seal atop a SCOG26 can be compromised in pressure swings or through mechanical damage (thus allowing the entry liquid contamination). Repeated pressure swings are thought to further drive contamination past a compromised seal.
- The calculated thermodynamic conditions within the SCOG26 accelerate the rate of gas generation beyond the capacity of the canister to contain the gases, despite pressure relief devices. The resulting non-equilibrium pressures can build to greater than 10,000 psi just prior to rupture.
- Testing shows that un-cracked candles contaminated with oil may not explode as violently as with cracked candles; however, the reaction can be rapid, violent, and potentially catastrophic.
- Heat, flame, noxious vapor formation, and propulsive action are all still possible even without container fragmentation.
- The overpressure damage reported from the Tireless mishap is well within that observed from a single contaminated SCOG26 device, and within the range of low explosives-like materials, including sodium chlorate plus oil based Sprengel-type explosives.
- No crater-like formations were reported, indicating a low probability of high-explosive behavior.

There are three distinct explosive events proposed to occur over the span of milliseconds:

1. Mechanical explosion due to contaminant-driven excessive gas generation in the container
2. BLEVE from (expansion of the now superheated) molten reactants and products following mechanical failure
3. VCE (or thermobaric) explosion of the vaporized oxidizer and fuel mixture

---

[1] *Development of a Solid Chlorate Backup Oxygen Delivery System for the International Space Station* (Graf, et. al.); SAE Technical Paper Series; 30th Intl. Conf. on Environmental Systems, Toulouse, France. July, 2000.

Testing provided direct evidence that mechanical and VCE-type explosions are possible under certain conditions, while BLEVE behavior is supported by the inferred pressure and temperature environment within the canister prior to bursting.

The videographic evidence suggests that all three types of explosive events were observed, though not all types were observed with every test. It is not possible to determine if all three types occurred during the Tireless mishap, though the tests which best represent the overall physical damage (fragmentation and mechanical damage to surrounding hardware) were characterized by the presence of all three types of explosive behavior.

7.2   Recommendations

- Pressure relief devices mitigate the explosion threat; however, no practical pressure relief device will remove the threat in a contaminated SCOG (due to choked flow through a relatively small opening). Instead, it is recommended that future designs intrinsically limit the capability of canisters to hold pressure (for example by sufficiently opening the ventilation path and changing the filtration media and its geometry).
- Testing should be conducted on proposed designs to validate their resistance to becoming contaminated (reducing risk by likelihood) and their tolerance to contamination (reducing risk by consequence).
- Reduce cracking through packaging and handling techniques and storage/stowage locations.
- Eliminate contamination through controlled processes from manufacture through use or disposal.
- Investigate mechanisms of in-process validation of cleanliness
- SCOG systems of any design should be treated like oxygen systems, with all affected personnel trained at the appropriate level in oxygen systems safety.

7.3   Root Cause Analysis and connections to the mishap described aboard HMS Tireless

In assessing the intrinsic vulnerability of CAN-26 based systems, with a particular focus on NASA's CAN-26-M system and similarities between it and the system believed to have been involved in the HMS Tireless mishap, Root Cause analysis (independent of this testing) was applied to identify potential routes to the explosive failure of such systems, regardless of probability. The exact circumstances of the Tireless Mishap may never be fully known; however, based on available data and materials the following are supposed:

- Hydrocarbon contamination was identified as the only credible mechanism providing the energy released in the reported mishap (Hydrocarbon contamination is seen as not likely aboard ISS).
- Cracking of the briquette was likely present.
- The vent paths and/or relief devices were likely clogged (in part or wholly).
- Due to the proposed mechanism of hydrocarbon introduction (namely leaking past compromised top seals) clogging is likely to accompany contamination due to other particulate material and/or liquids or humidity entering the SCOG26 and depositing in the filtration media or relief valves.
- No mechanisms or manufacturing defects were identified that were thought to reproduce the events of the mishap without the introduction of a foreign substance, which is theorized (because of its relative ubiquity aboard submarines) to have been a hydrocarbon liquid.
- The additional mechanisms of BLEVE and VCE can occur in this scenario, providing three distinct events, each independently capable of generating damaging overpressures.
- Fragment velocity estimates, based on photographic evidence, suggest ballistic velocities on the order of 1000 to 3000 ft/s were present. Both a mechanical explosion and a BLEVE can generate fragment velocities in this regime.

- VCE (thermobaric) effects would be external to the container and therefore not be the source of fragment acceleration.

7.4   Concluding Remark

Solid Fuel oxygenation offers several benefits over pressurized systems, both in terms of safety and equipment overhead. It is the opinion of the authors (supported by the data of this test series, previous test and validation campaigns and experience) that chlorate-based SCOG systems may be used safely provided the devices are free of contamination. Further risk reduction is achieved by creating intrinsically fault-tolerant designs accompanied with safe practices, robust procedural controls and in-process validations, where necessary. Chlorate-based oxygen systems should not be feared, but they do deserve the same respect and attention given to any oxygen system.

References

Beveridge, A., *Forensic Investigations of Explosions*, CRC Press LLC, Boca Raton, Florida 1998.

BOI. Board of Injury. *Circumstances Occurring March 20, 2007.* (Redacted) DEP2008-1531, Deposited Papers, House of Commons, Parliament, U.K., June 12, 2008.

Explosives Safety Standard, Air Force Manual 91-201, October 7, 1994.

Gibbs, T. R., and Popolato, A., LASL Explosives Property Data, University of California Press, Berkley-Los Angeles-London, 1980.

Gordon, S., and McBride, B.J., *Computer Program for Calculation of Complex Chemical Equilibrium Compositions, and Applications: Analysis,* NASA RP-1311 Part I, 1994.

Molecular Products, http://www.molecularproducts.com/technologies-chloratecandles.php, 2007.

Structures to Resist the Effects of Accidental Explosions, TM-1300 NAVPAC P-397 AFR 88-22, Department of the Army, the Navy and the Air Force, November 1994.

Development of a Solid Chlorate Backup Oxygen Delivery System for the International Space Station (Graf, et. al.); SAE Technical Paper Series; 30th Intl. Conf. on Environmental Systems, Toulouse, France. July, 2000.

CPSIA information can be obtained
at www.ICGtesting.com
Printed in the USA
BVOW09s0955040418
512450BV00010B/202/P

9 781289 102500